THE

SUNDAY SCHOOL

LITURGY.

"Let the high praises of God be in their mouth." — Ps. cxlix. 6.

THIRD EDITION.

BOSTON:
WALKER, WISE, AND COMPANY,
PUBLISHERS FOR THE
AMERICAN UNITARIAN ASSOCIATION,
21 Bromfield St.
1859.

University Press, Cambridge:
Printed by Welch, Bigelow, and Company.

PREFACE.

THIS Liturgy is designed to be used in the following manner.

At the opening of the school, the Superintendent will say: —

We will begin this service by reading Lesson numbered [name the number, and, after a moment's pause, the Superintendent will read the sentences marked "S.," and the Pupils the sentences marked "P.," alternately].

When this is read, the Superintendent will say: —

We will pray in the words of the Prayer numbered [name the number, and, after a moment's pause, the Superintendent will repeat each line, which will be repeated after him by the Pupils].

After this, the Superintendent will say: —

We will sing Hymn numbered [name the number, and read the Hymn, which will then be sung by the school].

At the close, he will say: —

We will close this session of the school by singing Hymn numbered [name the number].

The liturgical exercises are short, and, by changing the succession, a great variety may be secured. It is hoped that an observance of the method above named may give order, dignity, and impressiveness to the devotional services of the schools in which this book may be used.

Though giving less space than other similar publications to Natural Religion, and bringing into more prominence the great truths of the Gospel, and especially the need of a Redeemer, yet the book has no sectarian or dogmatic bias. It was prepared by a pastor who for years has consecrated scholarly and devout gifts to this interesting department of religious instruction. His manuscripts were examined by several gentlemen, who were requested to add, suppress, or recast portions, or entire parts, according to their judgment and taste. They gave time and care to this revision.

The work is now published under the joint approval of the Committees of the Sunday School Society and of the American Unitarian Association. Any suggestions with a view to its improvement will be gratefully received, as the only aim is to offer to the young the most attractive helps towards the end prayed for in the words of the motto, — "Let the high praises of God be in their mouth."

*a**

CONTENTS.

LESSONS.

PRAYERS.

HYMNS.

LESSONS.

1

LESSON I.

INVITATION TO WORSHIP.

S. The earth is the Lord's, and the fulness thereof; the world, and all they that dwell therein.

P. For he hath founded it upon the seas, and established it upon the floods.

S. Who shall ascend into the hill of the Lord? and who shall stand in his holy place?

P. He that hath clean hands, and a pure heart; who hath not lifted up his soul unto vanity, nor sworn deceitfully.

S. He shall receive the blessing from the Lord; and righteousness from the God of his salvation.

P. This is the generation of them that seek him; that seek thy face, O God of Jacob.

S. O come, let us sing unto the Lord; let us make a joyful noise to the Rock of our salvation.

P. Let us come before his presence with thanksgiving; and make a joyful noise unto him with psalms.

S. For the Lord is a great God; and a great King above all gods!

P. In his hand are the deep places of the earth; the strength of the hills is his also.

S. The sea is his, and he made it;

P. And his hands formed the dry land.

S. O come, let us worship, and bow down; and kneel before the Lord our Maker.

P. For he is our God; and we are the people of his pasture, and the sheep of his hand.

S. For the Lord is great, and greatly to be praised.

P. Honor and majesty are before him; strength and beauty are in his sanctuary.

S. Give unto the Lord, O ye kindred of the people, give unto the Lord glory and strength.

P. Give unto the Lord the glory due unto his name; bring an offering, and come into his courts.

S. O worship the Lord in the beauty of holiness; fear before him all the earth.

P. Say among the heathen, that the Lord reigneth! the world also shall be established, that it shall not be moved.

S. Let the heavens rejoice, and let the earth be glad; let the sea roar, and the fulness thereof.

P. Let the field be joyful, and all that is therein; let all the trees of the wood rejoice

S. Before the Lord; for he cometh, for he cometh to judge the earth. He shall judge the world with righteousness;

P. And the people with his truth.

LESSON II.

SEEKING GOD.

S. Give ear to my prayer, O God:

P. And hide not thyself from my supplication.

S. Attend unto me and hear me:

P. Be merciful unto me, for my soul trusteth in thee.

S. O God, thou art my God; early will I seek thee:

P. My soul thirsteth for thee, to see thy power and thy glory.

S. Because thy loving-kindness is better than life, my lips shall praise thee:

P. Thus will I bless thee while I live; I will lift up my hands in thy name.

S. My soul shall be satisfied, and my mouth shall praise thee with joyful lips:

P. When I remember thee on my bed, and meditate on thee in the night watches.

S. Because thou hast been my help:

P. Therefore in the shadow of thy wings will I rejoice.

S. My soul followeth hard after thee:

P. Thy right hand upholdeth me.

S. Be thou exalted, O God, above the heavens:

P. And let thy glory be above all the earth.

S. My heart is fixed, O God:

P. I will sing and give praise.

S. I will praise thee, O Lord, among the people.

P. I will sing unto thee among the nations.

S. For thy mercy is great unto the heavens:

P. And thy truth unto the clouds.

S. Be thou exalted, O God, above the heavens:

P. Let thy glory be above all the earth.

S. O give thanks unto the Lord; for he is good:

P. For his mercy endureth for ever.

LESSON III.

ASKING DIVINE INSTRUCTION.

S. Teach me, O Lord, the way of thy statutes, and I shall keep it unto the end.

P. Give me understanding, and I shall keep thy law; yea I shall observe it with my whole heart.

S. Make me to go in the path of thy commandments, for in that do I delight.

P. Incline my heart unto thy testimonies, and not to covetousness.

S. Turn away mine eyes from beholding vanity, and quicken thou me in thy way.

P. Establish thy word unto thy servant, who is devoted to thy fear.

S. Wherewith shall a young man cleanse his way?

P. By taking heed thereto, according to thy word.

S. With my whole heart have I sought thee:

P. O let me not wander from thy commandments.

S. Deal bountifully with thy servant, that I may live and keep thy word:

P. Open thou mine eyes, that I may behold wondrous things out of thy law.

S. Make me to understand the way of thy precepts:

P. So shall I talk of thy wondrous works.

S. Remove from me the way of lying, and grant me thy law graciously.

P. I have chosen the way of truth; thy judgments have I laid before me.

S. I have adhered unto thy testimonies: O Lord, put me not to shame.

P. I will run the way of thy commandments, when thou shalt enlarge my heart.

S. O give thanks unto the Lord; for he is good:

P. For his mercy endureth for ever.

LESSON IV.

O THAT MEN WOULD PRAISE THE LORD.

S. O that men would praise the Lord, for his goodness, and for his wonderful works to the children of men!

P. I will praise the Lord with my whole heart, in the assembly of the upright.

S. The works of the Lord are great:

P. Sought out of all them that have pleasure in them.

S. His work is honorable and glorious:

P. And his righteousness endureth for ever.

S. He hath made his wonderful works to be remembered:

P. The Lord is gracious and full of compassion.

S. He hath given meat unto them that fear him:

P. He will be ever mindful of his covenant.

S. The works of his hands are verity and judgment:

P. All his commandments are sure.

S. They stand for ever and ever, and are done in truth and uprightness:

P. He sent redemption unto his people.

S. He hath commanded his covenant for ever:

P. Holy and reverend is his name.

S. The fear of the Lord is the beginning of wisdom:

P. A good understanding have all they that do his commandments.

S. The Lord hath prepared his throne in the heavens:

P. And his kingdom ruleth over all.

S. Bless the Lord, ye his angels, that excel in strength:

P. That do his commandments, hearkening unto the voice of his word.

S. Bless ye the Lord, all ye his hosts:

P. Ye ministers of his, that do his pleasure.

S. Bless the Lord, all his works, in all places of his dominion:

P. Bless the Lord, O my soul.

LESSON V.

PRAISE FROM ALL GOD'S WORKS.

S. Praise ye the Lord; praise the Lord, O my soul! While I live, will I praise the Lord.

P. I will sing praises unto my God, while I have my being.

S. The Lord openeth the eyes of the blind; the Lord raiseth them that are bowed down:

P. The Lord loveth the righteous; the Lord preserveth the strangers.

S. He relieveth the fatherless and the widow; he healeth the broken in heart, and bindeth up their wounds.

P. Great is the Lord, and of great power; his understanding is infinite.

S. Sing unto the Lord with thanksgiving; sing praises upon the harp unto our God.

P. Praise ye the Lord, for it is good; for it is pleasant, and praise is comely.

S. Praise ye him, all his angels:

P. Praise him, all his hosts.

S. Praise ye him, sun and moon:

P. Praise him, all ye stars of light.

S. Praise him, ye heaven of heavens, and ye waters that be above the heavens.

P. Praise the Lord from the earth, fire and hail, snow and vapor, stormy wind, fulfilling his word:

S. Mountains, and all hills; fruitful trees, and all cedars;

P. Wild beasts, and all cattle, ye animals that creep, and birds that fly;

S. Kings of the earth, and all people; princes, and all judges of the earth; young men and maidens, old men and children:

P. Let them praise the name of the Lord.

S. For his name alone is excellent:

P. His glory is above the earth and heaven.

S. Praise him according to his excellent greatness.

P. For the Lord taketh pleasure in his people; he will beautify the meek with salvation:

S. Praise ye the Lord.

P. Sing praises unto our God; let every thing that hath breath praise the Lord.

LESSON VI.

GOD GREATLY TO BE PRAISED.

S. I will extol thee, my God, O King, and I will bless thy name for ever and ever.

P. Every day will I bless thee, and I will praise thy name for ever and ever.

S. Great is the Lord, and greatly to be praised; and his greatness is unsearchable.

P. One generation shall praise thy works to another, and shall declare thy mighty deeds.

S. I will speak of the glorious honor of thy majesty, and of thy wondrous works.

P. And men shall speak of the might of thy terrible acts; they shall abundantly utter the memory of thy great goodness, and shall sing of thy righteousness.

S. The Lord is gracious, and full of compassion; slow to anger, and of great mercy.

P. The Lord is good to all, and his tender mercies are over all his works.

S. All thy works shall praise thee, O Lord, and thy saints shall bless thee.

P. They shall speak of the glory of thy kingdom, and talk of thy power;

S. To make known to the sons of men thy mighty deeds, and the glorious majesty of thy kingdom.

P. Thy kingdom is an everlasting kingdom, and thy dominion endureth throughout all generations.

S. The Lord upholdeth all that fall;

P. And raiseth up all that be bowed down.

S. The eyes of all wait upon thee;

P. And thou givest them their meat in due season.

S. Thou openest thine hand;

P. And satisfiest the desire of every living thing.

S. The Lord is righteous in all his ways;

P. And holy in all his works.

S. The Lord is nigh unto all that call upon him;

P. To all that call upon him in truth.

S. He will fulfil the desire of them that fear

him; he will hear their cry, and will save them.

P. The Lord preserveth all them that love him.

S. My mouth shall speak the praise of the Lord;

P. And let all flesh bless his holy name, for ever and ever.

LESSON VII.

GOD SEEN IN HIS WORKS.

S. Bless the Lord, O my soul.

P. O Lord, my God, thou art very great; thou art clothed with honor and majesty.

S. Thou coverest thyself with light as with a garment; thou stretchest out the heavens like a curtain.

P. Thou layest the beams of thy chambers in the waters; thou makest the clouds thy chariot, and walkest upon the wings of the wind.

S. Thou makest the winds thy messengers, thy ministers the flaming fire.

P. Thou didst lay the foundations of the earth, that it should not be removed for ever.

S. The waters stood above the mountains; at thy rebuke they fled:

P. At the voice of thy thunder they hasted away.

S. Thou hast set a bound, that they may not pass over;

P. That they turn not to cover the earth.

S. Thou makest the grass to grow for the cattle;

P. And herb for the service of man.

S. Thou appointest the moon for seasons; the sun knoweth his going down.

P. O Lord, how manifold are thy works! In wisdom hast thou made them all.

S. The earth is full of thy riches;

P. So is this great and wide sea, wherein are things living innumerable.

S. These wait all upon thee, that thou mayest give them their meat in due season.

P. That thou givest them, they gather.

S. Thou openest thine hand;

P. They are filled with good.

S. Thou hidest thy face;

P. They are troubled.

S. Thou takest away their breath;

P. They die, and return to their dust.

S. Thou sendest forth thy spirit;

P. They are created, and thou renewest the face of the earth.

S. I will sing unto the Lord as long as I live; I will sing praise unto my God while I have my being.

P. My meditation of him shall be sweet; I will be glad in the Lord. Bless the Lord, O my soul!

LESSON VIII.

GOD'S WORKS AND WORD.

S. The heavens declare the glory of God, and the firmament showeth his handiwork.

P. Day unto day uttereth speech, and night unto night showeth knowledge.

S. They have no speech nor language, and their voice is not heard:

P. Yet their line is gone out through all the earth, and their words to the end of the world.

S. In them hath he set a tabernacle for the sun;

P. Which is as a bridegroom coming out of his chamber, and rejoiceth as a strong man to run a race.

S. His going forth is from the end of the heaven;

P. And his circuit unto the ends of it;

and there is nothing hid from the heat thereof.

S. The law of the Lord is perfect, converting the soul;

P. The testimony of the Lord is sure, making wise the simple:

S. The statutes of the Lord are right, rejoicing the heart;

P. The commandment of the Lord is pure, enlightening the eyes:

S. The fear of the Lord is clean, enduring for ever;

P. The judgments of the Lord are true, and righteous altogether:

S. More to be desired are they than gold; yea, than much fine gold:

P. Sweeter also than honey, and the honeycomb.

S. Moreover, by them is thy servant warned;

P. And in keeping of them there is great reward.

S. Who can understand his errors?

P. Cleanse thou me from secret faults!

S. Keep back thy servant also from presumptuous sins.

P. Let them not have dominion over me; then shall I be upright, and I shall be innocent from the great transgression.

S. Let the words of my mouth, and the meditation of my heart,

P. Be acceptable in thy sight, O Lord, my strength and my redeemer!

LESSON IX.

JOYFUL WORSHIP.

S. Make a joyful noise unto the Lord, all ye lands.

P. Serve the Lord with gladness; come before his presence with singing.

S. Know ye that the Lord, he is God; it is he that hath made us, and not we ourselves:

P. We are his people, and the sheep of his pasture.

S. Enter into his gates with thanksgiving, and into his courts with praise.

P. Be thankful unto him, and bless his name.

S. For the Lord is good; his mercy is everlasting,

P. And his truth endureth to all generations.

S. I was glad when they said unto me, Let us go into the house of the Lord.

P. Our feet shall stand within thy gates, O Jerusalem.

S. Pray for the peace of Jerusalem:

P. They shall prosper that love thee.

S. Peace be within thy walls;

P. And prosperity within thy palaces.

S. How amiable are thy tabernacles, O Lord of Hosts! My soul longeth, yea, even fainteth, for the courts of the Lord:

P. My heart and my flesh crieth out for the living God.

S. Yea, the sparrow hath found a house, and the swallow a nest for herself, where she may lay her young:

P. Even thine altars, O Lord of Hosts, my King and my God.

S. A day in thy courts is better than a thousand:

P. I would rather be a door-keeper in the house of my God, than to dwell in the tents of wickedness.

S. For the Lord God is a sun and shield; the Lord will give grace and glory:

P. No good thing will he withhold from them that walk uprightly.

S. Blessed are they that dwell in thy house; they will be still praising thee:

P. O Lord of Hosts, blessed is the man that trusteth in thee.

LESSON X.

REJOICING IN GOD.

S. I will sing of the mercies of the Lord for ever:

P. With my mouth will I make known thy faithfulness to all generations.

S. And the heavens shall praise thy wonders, O Lord:

P. Thy faithfulness also in the congregation of the saints.

S. For who, in the heaven, can be compared unto the Lord?

P. Who, among the sons of the mighty, can be likened unto the Lord?

S. God is greatly to be feared in the assembly of his saints:

P. And to be had in reverence of all them that are about him.

S. O Lord God of Hosts, who is a strong Lord, like unto thee?

P. Or to thy faithfulness round about thee?

S. Thou rulest the raging of the sea:

P. When the waves thereof arise, thou stillest them.

S. The heavens are thine, and the earth also is thine:

P. As for the world, and the fulness thereof, thou hast founded them.

S. The north and the south, thou hast created them:

P. Thou hast a mighty arm, and high is thy right hand.

S. Justice and judgment are the habitation of thy throne:

P. Mercy and truth shall go before thy face.

S. Blessed is the people that know the joyful sound:

P. They shall walk, O Lord, in the light of thy countenance.

S. In thy name shall they rejoice all the day:

P. And in thy righteousness shall they be exalted.

S. For the Lord is our defence:

P. And the Holy One of Israel is our king.

S. O give thanks unto the Lord; for he is good:

P. For his mercy endureth for ever.

LESSON XI.

THE GOODNESS OF GOD.

S. I will bless the Lord at all times; his praise shall continually be in my mouth.

P. O magnify the Lord with me, and let us exalt his name together.

S. I sought the Lord, and he heard me, and delivered me from all my fears.

P. Look up unto him and be enlightened, and your faces shall never be ashamed.

S. The poor man cried, and the Lord heard him, and saved him out of all his troubles.

P. The angel of the Lord encampeth round about them that fear him, and delivereth them.

S. O taste and see that the Lord is good:

P. Blessed is the man that trusteth in him.

S. O fear the Lord, ye his saints; for there is no want to them that fear him.

P. The young lions do lack, and suffer hunger; but they that seek the Lord shall not want any good thing.

S. Come, ye children, hearken unto me; I will teach you the fear of the Lord.

P. What man is he that desireth life, and loveth many days, that he may see good?

S. Keep thy tongue from evil, and thy lips from speaking guile:

P. Depart from evil, and do good; seek peace, and pursue it.

S. The eyes of the Lord are upon the righteous, and his ears are open unto their cry:

P. The face of the Lord is against them that do evil, to cut off the remembrance of them from the earth.

S. The righteous cry, and the Lord heareth, and delivereth them out of all their troubles.

P. The Lord is nigh unto them that are of a broken heart, and saveth such as be of a contrite spirit.

S. Evil shall slay the wicked; and they that hate the righteous shall be desolate.

P. The Lord redeemeth the soul of his servants, and none of them that trust in him shall be desolate.

LESSON XII.

THE CREATION.

S. In the beginning, God created the heaven and the earth.

P. And the earth was without form and void, and darkness was upon the face of the deep; and the spirit of God moved upon the face of the waters.

S. And God said, Let there be light; and there was light:

P. And God saw the light that it was good.

S. And God said, Let the waters under the heaven be gathered together unto one place, and let the dry land appear:

P. And it was so.

S. And God said, Let the earth bring forth grass, the herb yielding seed, and the fruit-tree yielding fruit:

P. And it was so; and God saw that it was good.

S. And God created every living creature that moveth in the waters, which brought forth abundantly, and every winged fowl:

P. And God saw that it was good, and blessed them.

S. And God made the beast of the earth, and cattle, and every thing that creepeth upon the earth:

P. And God saw that it was good.

S. And God said, Let us make man in our image, after our likeness; and let him have dominion over the fish of the sea and the fowl of the air, and the cattle, and over all the earth, and over every creeping thing that creepeth upon the earth:

P. So God created man in his own image, and blessed him; and God saw everything that he had made, and behold it was very good.

S. O Lord, our God, how excellent is thy name in all the earth! When I consider the heavens, the work of thy fingers;

P. The moon and the stars which thou hast ordained,

S. What is man that thou art mindful of him,

P. And the son of man that thou visitest him?

S. For thou hast made him a little lower than the angels,

P. And hast crowned him with glory and honor.

S. Thou madest him to have dominion over all the works of thy hand.

P. O Lord, our Lord, how excellent is thy name in all the earth!

LESSON XIII.

GOD EVER PRESENT.

S. O Lord, thou hast searched me and known me.

P. Thou knowest my down-sitting and mine uprising; thou understandest my thought afar off.

S. Thou compassest my path and my lying down, and art acquainted with all my ways.

P. For there is not a word in my tongue, but lo! O Lord, thou knowest it altogether.

S. Thou hast beset me behind and before, and laid thine hand upon me.

P. Such knowledge is too wonderful for me; it is high; I cannot attain unto it.

S. Whither shall I go from thy spirit? or whither shall I flee from thy presence?

P. If I ascend up into heaven, thou art there; if I make my bed in the grave, behold thou art there.

S. If I take the wings of the morning, and dwell in the uttermost parts of the sea,

P. Even there shall thy hand lead me, and thy right hand shall hold me.

S. If I say, Surely the darkness shall cover me, even the night shall be light about me.

P. Yea, the darkness hideth not from thee; but the night shineth as the day. The darkness and the light are both alike to thee.

S. I will praise thee, for I am fearfully and wonderfully made.

P. Marvellous are thy works, and that my soul knoweth right well.

S. How precious also are thy thoughts unto me, O God! How great is the sum of them!

P. If I should count them, they are more in number than the sand; when I awake, I am still with thee.

S. Search me, O God, and know my heart;

P. Try me, and know my thoughts;

S. And see if there be any wicked way in me,

P. And lead me in the way everlasting.

LESSON XIV.

GOD HEARING PRAYER.

S. The Lord is nigh unto all them that call upon him, to all that call upon him in truth:

P. He will fulfil the desires of them that fear him; he will hear their cry, and will save them.

S. If I regard iniquity in my heart, the Lord will not hear me.

P. The sacrifice of the wicked is an abomination to the Lord, but the prayer of the upright is his delight.

S. He that cometh to God must believe that he is, and that he is a rewarder of them that diligently seek him.

P. And ye shall seek me and find me, saith the Lord, when ye shall search for me with all your heart.

S. The hour cometh, and now is, when the true worshippers shall worship the Father in spirit and in truth;

P. For the Father seeketh such to worship him.

S. Ask, and it shall be given you; seek, and ye shall find; knock, and it shall be opened unto you.

P. For every one that asketh, receiveth; and he that seeketh, findeth; and to him that knocketh, it shall be opened.

S. When thou prayest, enter into thy closet; and when thou hast shut thy door, pray to thy Father which is in secret;

P. And thy Father, which seeth in secret, shall reward thee openly.

S. If any of you lack wisdom, let him ask of God, that giveth to all men liberally and upbraideth not,

P. And it shall be given him.

S. After this manner, therefore, pray ye:

The Pupils repeating after the Superintendent.

Our Father who art in heaven,
Hallowed be thy name;
Thy kingdom come;
Thy will be done on earth as it is in heaven.

Give us this day our daily bread;
And forgive us our debts as we forgive our debtors;
And lead us not into temptation, but deliver us from evil;
For thine is the kingdom, and the power, and the glory, for ever. Amen.

LESSON XV.

THE HEAVENLY REFUGE.

S. He that dwelleth in the secret place of the Most High shall abide under the shadow of the Almighty.

P. I will say of the Lord, he is my refuge and my fortress; my God, in him will I trust.

S. Surely he shall deliver thee from the snare of the fowler, and from the noisome pestilence.

P. He shall cover thee with his feathers, and under his wings shalt thou trust.

S. Thou shalt not be afraid for the terror by night, nor for the arrow that flieth by day;

P. Nor for the pestilence that walketh in darkness, nor for the destruction that wasteth at noonday.

S. A thousand shall fall at thy side, and ten thousand at thy right hand; but it shall not come nigh thee.

4

P. Only with thine eyes shalt thou behold, and see the reward of the wicked.

S. Because thou hast made the Lord thy refuge, even the Most High thy habitation,

P. There shall no evil befall thee; neither shall any plague come nigh thy dwelling;

S. For he shall give his angels charge over thee, to keep thee in all thy ways.

P. They shall bear thee up in their hands, lest thou dash thy foot against a stone:

S. Thou shalt tread upon the lion and adder; the young lion and the dragon shalt thou trample under feet.

P. Because he hath set his love upon me, will I deliver him: I will set him on high, because he hath known my name.

S. He shall call upon me, and I will answer him; I will be with him in trouble; I will deliver him and honor him.

P. With long life will I satisfy him, and show him my salvation.

LESSON XVI.

CONFIDENCE IN THE DIVINE PROTECTION.

S. Delight thyself in the Lord, and he shall give thee the desires of thine heart.

P. Commit thy way unto the Lord; trust also in him, and he shall bring it to pass.

S. Rest in the Lord, and wait patiently for him; fret not thyself because of him who prospereth in his way; because of the man who bringeth wicked devices to pass.

P. Cease from anger, and forsake wrath; fret not thyself in anywise to do evil; for evil-doers shall be cut off.

S. A little that a righteous man hath, is better than the riches of many wicked:

P. The Lord knoweth the days of the upright; they shall not be ashamed in the evil time.

S. The steps of a good man are ordered by the Lord:

P. Though he fall, he shall not be utterly cast down; for the Lord upholdeth him with his hand.

S. I have been young, and now am old; yet have I not seen the righteous forsaken, nor his seed begging bread.

P. Depart from evil and do good, and dwell for evermore.

S. For the Lord loveth judgment, and forsaketh not his saints.

P. The mouth of the righteous speaketh wisdom, and his tongue talketh of judgment.

S. The law of his God is in his heart; none of his steps shall slide. I have seen the wicked in great power, and spreading himself, like a green bay-tree;

P. Yet he passed away; and lo! he was not; yea, I sought him, but he could not be found!

S. Mark the perfect man, and behold the upright; for the end of that man is peace!

P. The salvation of the righteous is of the

Lord; hè is their strength in the time of trouble.

S. And the Lord shall help them, and deliver them; he shall deliver them from the wicked,

P. Because they trust in him.

LESSON XVII.

GOD OUR KEEPER.

S. I will lift up mine eyes unto the hills, from whence cometh my help.

P. My help cometh from the Lord, which made heaven and earth.

S. He will not suffer thy foot to be moved; he that keepeth thee will not slumber:

P. He that keepeth Israel shall neither slumber nor sleep.

S. The Lord is thy keeper; the Lord is thy shade upon thy right hand.

P. The sun shall not smite thee by day, nor the moon by night.

S. The Lord shall preserve thee from all evil; he shall preserve thy soul.

P. The Lord shall preserve thy going out and thy coming in, from this time forth, and even for evermore.

S. I love the Lord, because he hath heard my voice and my supplications.

P. Because he hath inclined his ear unto me, and heard me; therefore will I call upon him as long as I live.

S. Gracious is the Lord, and righteous; yea, our God is merciful.

P. The Lord preserveth the simple; I was brought low, and he helped me.

S. Return unto thy rest, O my soul, for the Lord hath dealt bountifully with thee.

P. For thou hast delivered my soul from death, my eyes from tears, and my feet from falling.

S. I will walk before the Lord in the land of the living.

P. I will offer to thee the sacrifices of thanksgiving, and will call upon the name of the Lord.

S. O praise the Lord, all ye nations; praise him, all ye people;

P. For his merciful kindness is great toward us; and the truth of the Lord endureth for ever. Praise ye the Lord.

LESSON XVIII.

THE DIVINE SHEPHERD.

S. The Lord is my Shepherd, I shall not want.

P. He maketh me to lie down in green pastures; he leadeth me beside the still waters:

S. He restoreth my soul; he leadeth me in the paths of righteousness for his name's sake.

P. Yea, though I walk through the valley of the shadow of death, I will fear no evil:

S. For thou art with me; thy rod and thy staff they comfort me.

P. Thou preparest a table before me in the presence of mine enemies.

S. Thou anointest my head with oil; my cup runneth over.

P. Surely goodness and mercy shall follow me all the days of my life, and I will dwell in the house of the Lord for ever.

S. Give ear, O Shepherd of Israel, thou that leadest Joseph like a flock; thou that dwellest between the cherubim, shine forth.

P. Turn us again, O God, and cause thy face to shine upon us, and we shall be saved.

LESSON XIX.

TENDERNESS OF THE DIVINE LOVE

S. Bless the Lord, O my soul, and all that is within me bless his holy name.

P. Bless the Lord, O my soul, and forget not all his benefits;

S. Who forgiveth all thine iniquities; who healeth all thy diseases;

P. Who redeemeth thy life from destruction; who crowneth thee with loving-kindness and tender mercies;

S. Who satisfieth thy mouth with good, so that thy youth is renewed like the eagle's.

P. The Lord executeth righteousness and judgment for all that are oppressed.

S. He made known his ways unto Moses; his acts unto the children of Israel.

P. The Lord is merciful and gracious; slow to anger, and plenteous in mercy.

S. He will not always chide; neither will he keep his anger for ever.

P. He hath not dealt with us after our sins, nor rewarded us according to our iniquities.

S. For as the heaven is high above the earth, so great is his mercy toward them that fear him.

P. As far as the east is from the west, so far hath he removed our transgressions from us.

S. Like as a father pitieth his children, so the Lord pitieth them that fear him.

P. For he knoweth our frame; he remembereth that we are dust.

S. As for man, his days are as grass; as a flower of the field, so he flourisheth;

P. For the wind passeth over it, and it is gone; and the place thereof shall know it no more.

S. But the mercy of the Lord is from everlasting to everlasting upon them that fear him;

P. And his righteousness unto children's children to such as keep his covenant, and to those that remember his commandments to do them.

S. The Lord hath prepared his throne in

the heavens, and his kingdom ruleth over all.

P. His kindgom is an everlasting kingdom, and his dominion endureth throughout all generations.

S. Bless the Lord, ye his angels, that excel in strength, that do his commandments, hearkening unto the voice of his word.

P. Bless the Lord, all ye his hosts; ye ministers of his, that do his pleasure.

S. Bless the Lord, all his works, in all places of his dominion:

P. Bless the Lord, O my soul!

LESSON XX.

GOD ORDERING OUR WAYS.

S. Blessed are the undefiled in the way:

P. Who walk in the law of the Lord.

S. Blessed are they that keep his testimonies:

P. And that seek him with the whole heart.

S. O that my ways were directed to keep thy statutes!

P. Then shall I not be ashamed, when I have respect unto all thy commandments.

S. I will praise thee with uprightness of heart:

P. When I shall have learned thy righteous judgments.

S. I will keep thy statutes:

P. O forsake me not utterly.

S. I will never forget thy precepts:

P. For with them thou hast quickened me.

S. How sweet are thy words unto my taste!

P. Yea, sweeter than honey to my mouth.

S. Through thy precepts I get understanding:

P. Therefore I hate every false way.

S. Deal with thy servant according to thy mercy:

P. I am thy servant; give me understanding, that I may know thy testimonies.

S. Quicken me, O Lord, according to thy word:

P. Accept, I beseech thee, the free-will offerings of my mouth, O Lord.

S. O give thanks unto the Lord; for he is good:

P. For his mercy endureth for ever.

LESSON XXI.

DEVOUT TRUST.

S. The Lord is my light and my salvation; whom shall I fear?

P. The Lord is the strength of my life; of whom shall I be afraid?

S. Though a host should encamp against me, my heart shall not fear;

P. For in the time of trouble, he shall hide me in his pavilion.

S. Hear, O Lord, when I cry with my voice; have mercy upon me, and answer me.

P. When thou saidst, Seek ye my face; my heart said unto thee, Thy face, Lord, will I seek.

S. Leave me not, neither forsake me, O God of my salvation.

P. When my father and my mother forsake me, then the Lord will take me up.

S. Teach me thy way, O Lord, and lead me in a plain path:

P. I had fainted, unless I had believed to see the goodness of the Lord in the land of the living:

S. Wait on the Lord:

P. Be of good courage, and he shall strengthen thy heart.

S. Blessed be the Lord, because he hath heard the voice of my supplication.

P. The Lord is my strength and my shield.

S. My heart trusted in him, and I am helped:

P. Therefore my heart greatly rejoiceth, and with my song will I praise him.

S. Give unto the Lord, O ye mighty! give unto the Lord glory and strength.

P. Give unto the Lord the glory due unto his name; worship the Lord in the beauty of holiness.

S. The voice of the Lord is powerful:

P. The voice of the Lord is full of majesty.

S. The voice of the Lord divideth the flames of fire.

P. The Lord shaketh the wilderness: the Lord sitteth upon the flood.

S. Yea, the Lord sitteth king for ever:

P. The Lord will bless his people with peace.

LESSON XXII.

HUMAN FRAILTY AND THE DIVINE HELP.

S. Lord, make me to know mine end, and the measure of my days, what it is;

P. That I may know how frail I am.

S. Behold, thou hast made my days as a handbreadth, and mine age is as nothing before thee:

P. Every man at his best estate is altogether vanity.

S. Thou hast been our dwelling-place in all generations. Before the mountains were brought forth, or ever thou hadst formed the earth and the world,

P. Even from everlasting to everlasting, thou art God.

S. Thou turnest man to destruction; and sayest, Return, ye children of men.

P. For a thousand years in thy sight are but as yesterday when it is past, and as a watch in the night.

S. Thou carriest them away as with a flood:

P. They are as a sleep.

S. They are like grass, which groweth up in the morning;

P. And in the evening is cut down and withereth.

S. God is our refuge and strength:

P. A very present help in trouble.

S. Therefore will we not fear, though the earth be removed;

P. And though the mountains be carried into the midst of the sea.

S. I waited patiently for the Lord; and he inclined unto me, and heard my cry.

P. And he hath put a new song in my mouth, even praise unto our God.

S. Blessed is the man that maketh the Lord his trust;

P. And respecteth not the proud, nor such as turn aside unto lies.

S. Many, O Lord, are thy wonderful works, and thy thoughts which are to us ward.

P. If I would declare and speak of them, they are more than can be numbered.

S. I delight to do thy will, O my God; yea, thy law is within my heart.

P. Let thy loving-kindness and thy truth continually preserve me: let those that seek thee rejoice, and be glad in thee.

S. God is our guide, for ever and ever:

P. He will be our guide, even unto death.

LESSON XXIII.

CONFESSION OF SINS.

S. Have mercy upon me, O Lord, according to thy loving-kindness; according to the multitude of thy tender mercies, blot out my transgressions.

P. Wash me thoroughly from mine iniquity, and cleanse me from my sin:

S. For I acknowledge my transgression, and my sin is ever before me.

P. Behold, thou desirest truth in the inward parts, and in the hidden part thou shalt make me to know wisdom.

S. Create in me a clean heart, O God, and renew a right spirit within me.

P. Cast me not away from thy presence; and take not thy holy spirit from me.

S. O Lord, open thou my lips;

P. And my mouth shall show forth thy praise.

S. For thou desirest not sacrifice, else would

I give it; thou delightest not in burnt-offerings.

P. The sacrifices of God are a broken spirit: a broken and a contrite heart thou wilt not despise.

S. Seek ye the Lord while he may be found; call ye upon him while he is near. Let the wicked forsake his way, and the unrighteous man his thoughts;

P. And let him return unto the Lord, and he will have mercy upon him; and to our God, for he will abundantly pardon.

S. For my thoughts are not your thoughts, neither are your ways my ways, saith the Lord.

P. For as the heavens are higher than the earth, so are my ways higher than your ways, and my thoughts than your thoughts.

S. For thus saith the high and lofty One that inhabiteth eternity, whose name is Holy: I dwell in the high and holy place;

P. With him also that is of a contrite and humble spirit; to revive the spirit of the humble, and to revive the heart of the contrite.

LESSON XXIV.

IMPLORING MERCY.

S. Bow down thine ear, O Lord, and hear me:

P. Preserve my soul; O thou my God, save thy servant, that trusteth in thee.

S. Be merciful unto me, O Lord, for I cry unto thee daily:

P. Rejoice the soul of thy servant; for unto thee, O Lord, do I lift up my soul.

S. For thou, Lord, art good, and ready to forgive:

P. And plenteous in mercy to all them that call upon thee.

S. Give ear, O Lord, to my prayer:

P. And attend to the voice of my supplications.

S. Teach me thy way, O Lord:

P. I will walk in thy truth: unite my heart to fear thy name.

S. I will praise thee, O Lord, my God, with all my heart:

P. And I will glorify thy name for ever.

S. For great is thy mercy towards me:

P. And thou hast delivered my soul.

S. Thou, O Lord, art a God full of compassion, and gracious; long-suffering, and plenteous in mercy and truth:

P. Show us thy mercy, O Lord, and grant us thy salvation.

S. Thou hast holden me by my right hand:

P. Thou shalt guide me with thy counsel, and afterward receive me to glory.

S. Whom have I in heaven but thee?

P. And there is none upon earth that I desire beside thee.

S. My flesh and my heart fail:

P. But God is the strength of my heart, and my portion for ever.

S. For lo! they that are far from thee shall perish:

P. Thou hast destroyed all them that go astray from thee.

S. But it is good for me to draw near to God:

P. I have put my trust in the Lord God, that I may declare all thy works.

S. O give thanks unto the Lord; for he is good:

P. For his mercy endureth for ever.

LESSON XXV.

CHOOSING GOD FOR OUR PORTION.

S. Thou art my portion, O Lord:

P. I have said that I would keep thy words.

S. I entreated thy favor with my whole heart:

P. Be merciful unto me, according to thy word.

S. I thought on my ways, and turned my feet unto thy testimonies:

P. Behold, I have longed after thy precepts; quicken me in thy righteousness

S. I have remembered thy name, O Lord, in the night, and have kept thy law:

P. At midnight I will rise to give thanks unto thee, because of thy righteous judgments.

S. The earth, O Lord, is full of thy mercy:

P. Thou hast dealt well with thy servant, O Lord, according unto thy word.

S. Thy hands have made me and fashioned me:

P. Give me understanding, that I may learn thy commandments.

S. Let thy merciful kindness be for my comfort, according to thy word:

P. Let thy tender mercies come unto me, that I may live; for thy law is my delight.

S. Let those that fear thee turn unto me, and those that have known thy testimonies:

P. Let my heart be sound in thy statutes, that I be not ashamed.

S. O give thanks unto the Lord; for he is good:

P. For his mercy endureth for ever.

LESSON XXVI.

LOOKING UP FOR HELP.

S. Unto thee I lift up mine eyes, O Thou who dwellest in the heavens:

P. As the eyes of servants look to the hand of their masters, so our eyes wait upon the Lord our God, until he have mercy upon us.

S. It is of the Lord's mercies that we are not consumed, because his compassions fail not.

P. They are new every morning: great is thy faithfulness.

S. The Lord is my portion; therefore will I hope in him:

P. The Lord is good to them that wait for him; to the soul that seeketh him.

S. While I live will I praise the Lord:

P. I will sing praises to my God while I have any being.

S. Happy is he whose hope is in the Lord his God:

P. Who made heaven and earth, the sea, and all that therein is:

S. Who keepeth truth for ever:

P. Who executeth judgment for the oppressed.

S. The Lord looseth the prisoners: the Lord openeth the eyes of the blind:

P. The Lord raiseth them that are bowed down:

S. The Lord preserveth the strangers; he relieveth the fatherless and the widow:

P. But the way of the wicked he turneth upside down.

S. The Lord taketh pleasure in his people; he will beautify the meek with salvation.

P. Let the saints be joyful in glory; let the high praises of God be in their mouth.

S. O give thanks unto the Lord; for he is good:

P. For his mercy endureth for ever.

LESSON XXVII.

HOPE IN TROUBLE.

S. Out of the depths have I cried unto thee, O Lord:

P. Lord, hear my voice; let thine ears be attentive to the voice of my supplications.

S. If thou, Lord, shouldst mark iniquities, O Lord, who shall stand?

P. But there is forgiveness with thee, that thou mayest be feared.

S. I wait for the Lord; my soul doth wait, and in his word do I hope:

P. My soul waiteth for the Lord more than they that watch for the morning.

S. With the Lord there is mercy, and with him is plenteous redemption.

P. Lord, I have hoped for thy salvation, and done thy commandments.

S. My soul hath kept thy testimonies, and I love them exceedingly:

P. I have kept thy precepts and thy testimonies, for all my ways are before thee.

S. Let my cry come near before thee, O Lord; give me understanding, according to thy word:

P. Let my supplication come before thee; deliver me, according to thy word.

S. My lips shall utter praise, when thou hast taught me thy statutes:

P. My tongue shall speak of thy word; for all thy commandments are righteousness.

S. Let thy hand help thee; for I have chosen thy precepts.

P. I have longed for thy salvation, O Lord; and thy law is my delight.

S. Let my soul live, and it shall praise thee:

P. Let thy judgments help thee, for I do not forget thy commandments.

LESSON XXVIII.

CHRISTIAN LOVE.

S. God is love; and he that dwelleth in love, dwelleth in God, and God in him.

P. No man hath seen God at any time: if we love one another, God dwelleth in us, and his love is perfected in us.

S. He that loveth not his brother, whom he hath seen, how can he love God, whom he hath not seen?

P. And this commandment have we from Him, that he who loveth God, love his brother also.

S. Pure religion and undefiled before God and the Father is this:

P. To visit the fatherless and widows in their affliction, and to keep himself unspotted from the world.

S. Recompense to no man evil for evil.

P. Bless them which persecute you.

S. If it be possible, as much as lieth in you, live peaceably with all men.

P. If thine enemy hunger, feed him; if he thirst, give him drink. Be not overcome of evil, but overcome evil with good.

S. Let every man be swift to hear, slow to speak; slow to wrath, for the wrath of man worketh not the righteousness of God.

P. Let all bitterness and wrath and clamor and evil-speaking be put away from you, with all malice:

S. And be ye kind one to another, tender-hearted, forgiving one another, even as God, through Christ, hath forgiven you.

P. Be ye, therefore, followers of God, as dear children.

S. And the peace of God, which passeth all understanding, shall keep your hearts and minds through Christ Jesus.

P. Now unto him that is able to keep us from falling, and to present us faultless before the presence of his glory with exceeding joy;

S. Unto him that is able to do exceeding abundantly above all that we can ask or think;

P. Unto him be glory in the church, through Christ Jesus, world without end. Amen.

LESSON XXIX.

THE FUTURE LIFE.

S. In my Father's house, said Jesus, are many mansions; if it were not so, I would have told you. I go to prepare a place for you:

P. And if I go to prepare a place for you, I will come again, and receive you unto myself, that where I am, there ye may be also.

S. Yet a little while, the world seeth me no more; but ye see me:

P. Because I live, ye shall live also.

S. I am the resurrection and the life; he that believeth in me, though he were dead, yet shall he live:

P. And whosoever liveth and believeth in me, shall never die.

S. He that heareth my word, and believeth on Him that sent me, hath everlasting life;

P. And shall not come into condemnation, but is passed from death unto life.

S. It is sown in corruption; it is raised in incorruption.

P. It is sown in dishonor; it is raised in glory.

S. It is sown in weakness; it is raised in power.

P. It is sown a natural body; it is raised a spiritual body.

S. And, as we have borne the image of the earthy, we shall also bear the image of the heavenly.

P. For this corruptible must put on incorruption, and this mortal must put on immortality.

S. So when this corruptible shall have put on incorruption, and this mortal shall have put on immortality,

P. Then shall be brought to pass the saying that is written, Death is swallowed up in victory.

S. O death, where is thy sting? O grave, where is thy victory?

P. The sting of death is sin; but thanks be to God which giveth us the victory, through our Lord Jesus Christ.

S. Therefore, my beloved brethren, be ye steadfast, immovable, always abounding in the work of the Lord;

P. Forasmuch as ye know that your labor is not in vain in the Lord.

LESSON XXX.

RETRIBUTION.

S. The Lord shall endure for ever; he hath prepared his throne for judgment; he shall judge the world in righteousness, and minister judgment to the people in uprightness.

P. And we are sure that the judgment of God is according to truth, who will render to every man according to his deeds:

S. To them who, by patient continuance in well-doing, seek for glory, honor, and immortality,

P. Eternal life;

S. But unto them that are contentious, and do not obey the truth,

P. Indignation and wrath, tribulation and anguish, upon every soul of man that doeth evil.

S. But glory, honor, and peace to every man that worketh good.

P. For there is no respect of persons with God; for not the hearers of the law are just before God, but the doers of the law shall be justified.

S. I beseech you, therefore, by the mercies of God, that ye present your bodies a living sacrifice, holy, acceptable unto God, which is your reasonable service.

P. And be not conformed to this world; but be ye transformed by the renewing of your mind,

S. That ye may prove what is that good and acceptable and perfect will of God.

P. For none of us liveth to himself, and no man dieth to himself.

S. But whether we live, we live unto the Lord; or whether we die, we die unto the Lord.

P. Whether we live, therefore, or die, we are the Lord's.

S. As I live, saith the Lord, every knee shall bow to me, and every tongue shall confess to God.

P. So, then, every one of us shall give account of himself to God.

S. But eye hath not seen, nor ear heard,

neither hath entered into the heart of man,

P. The things which God hath prepared for them that love him.

S. O the depth of the riches, both of the wisdom and knowledge of God!

P. How unsearchable are his judgments, and his ways past finding out!

LESSON XXXI.

THE COMMANDMENTS.

S. Fear God and keep his commandments; for this is the whole duty of man.

P. For God shall bring every work into judgment, with every secret thing, whether it be good or whether it be evil.

S. He hath showed thee, O man, what is good.

P. What doth the Lord require of thee but to do justly, love mercy, and walk humbly with thy God?

S. God is no respecter of persons;

P. But in every nation he that feareth him and worketh righteousness is accepted with him.

S. He that hath my commandments and keepeth them, he it is that loveth me, said the Saviour;

P. And he that loveth me, shall be loved of my Father; and I will love him, and will manifest myself to him.

S. The first of all the commandments is this:

P. Thou shalt love the Lord thy God with all thy heart, and with all thy soul, and with all thy mind, and with all thy strength.

S. And the second is like unto it; namely, this:

P. Thou shalt love thy neighbor as thyself: there is none other commandment greater than these.

S. And one came, and said unto Jesus, What good thing shall I do that I may have eternal life?

P. And Jesus said unto him, Keep the commandments:

S. Thou shalt do no murder; thou shalt not commit adultery;

P. Thou shalt not steal; thou shalt not bear false witness;

S. Honor thy father and thy mother; and thou shalt love thy neighbor as thyself.

P. If ye keep my commandments, said Jesus, ye shall abide in my love, even as I have kept my Father's commandments, and abide in his love.

S. Know ye not, that to whom ye yield yourselves servants to obey, his servants ye are whom ye obey?

P. For the wages of sin is death, but the gift of God is eternal life, through Jesus Christ our Lord.

S. Now the end of the commandment is charity out of a pure heart, and of a good conscience, and of faith unfeigned.

P. Come unto me, said Jesus, all ye that labor and are heavy laden, and I will give you rest.

S. Take my yoke upon you, and learn of me; for I am meek and lowly in heart, and ye shall find rest to your souls;

P. For my-yoke is easy, and my burden is light.

LESSON XXXII.

LOVE FOR CHRIST.

S. I am the true vine; and my Father is the husbandman.

P. Every branch in me that beareth not fruit he taketh away; and every branch that beareth fruit, he purgeth it that it may bring forth more fruit.

S. Abide in me, and I in you; as the branch cannot bear fruit of itself except it abide in the vine, no more can ye, except ye abide in me.

P. I am the vine, ye are the branches. He that abideth in me, the same bringeth forth much fruit.

S. If ye abide in me, and my words abide in you, ye shall ask what ye will, and it shall be done unto you.

P. Herein is my father glorified, that ye bear much fruit; so shall ye be my disciples.

S. As the Father hath loved me, so have I loved you; continue ye in my love.

P. If ye keep my commandments, ye shall abide in my love, even as I have kept my Father's commandments, and abide in his love.

S. Greater love hath no man than this, that a man lay down his life for his friend:

P. Ye are my friends, if ye do whatsoever I command you.

S. A new commandment I give unto you, that ye love one another; as I have loved you, that ye also love one another.

P. By this shall all men know that ye are my disciples, if ye have love one to another.

S. He that loveth his brother abideth in the light, and there is no occasion of stumbling in him.

P. He that hateth his brother walketh in darkness, and knoweth not whither he goeth, because the darkness hath blinded his eyes.

S. God is love; and he that dwelleth in love dwelleth in God, and God in him.

P. There is no fear in love; but perfect love casteth out fear.

S. He that loveth not his brother, whom he hath seen, how can he love God, whom he hath not seen?

P. And this commandment have we from Him, that he who loveth God, love his brother also.

LESSON XXXIII.

THE DIVINE MISSION OF CHRIST.

S. And Jesus, when he was baptized, went up straightway out of the water, and lo! the heavens were opened unto him, and he saw the Spirit of God descending like a dove, and lighting upon him.

P. And lo! a voice from heaven saying, This is my beloved Son, in whom I am well pleased.

S. Art thou he that should come, or do we look for another?

P. The blind receive their sight, and the lame walk; the lepers are cleansed, and the deaf hear; the dead are raised up, and the poor have the gospel preached to them; and blessed is he whosoever shall not be offended in me.

S. Whom say ye that I am?

P. Thou art the Christ, the Son of the living God.

S. The Word was made flesh and dwelt among us, and we beheld his glory;

P. The glory as of the only begotten of the Father, full of grace and truth.

S. The Son can do nothing of himself, but what he seeth the Father do; for whatsoever the Father doeth, that also doeth the Son likewise.

P. For the Father loveth the Son, and showeth him all things that himself doeth.

S. I can of mine own self do nothing; as I hear I judge; and my judgment is just, because I seek not mine own will, but the will of the Father who sent me.

P. All authority is given unto me of my Father.

S. I am come in my Father's name. The works which the Father hath given me to finish, the same works that I do, bear witness of me that the Father hath sent me.

P. And the Father himself who hath sent me hath borne witness to me.

S. I came down from heaven, not to do mine own will, but the will of Him that sent me.

P. And this is the will of Him that sent me, that every one who seeth the Son and believeth on him may have everlasting life.

S. My doctrine is not mine, but His who sent me. If any man will do His will, he shall know of the doctrine, whether it be of God, or whether I speak of myself.

P. He that seeketh His glory that sent him, the same is true, and no unrighteousness is in him.

S. I have not spoken of myself; but the Father who sent me, he gave me a commandment what I should say, and what I should speak.

P. And we know that his commandment is life everlasting.

S. Believe me that I am in the Father, and the Father in me; or else believe me for the very works' sake.

P. He that believeth on me, the works that I do shall he do also; and greater works than these shall he do, because I go unto my Father.

S. At that day ye shall know that I am

in my Father, and ye in me, and I in you.

P. For he that loveth me shall be loved of my Father, and we will come unto him, and make our abode with him.

S. These are written that ye might believe that Jesus is the Christ, the Son of God.

P. And that, believing, ye might have life through his name.

LESSON XXXIV.

OFFICES OF THE SAVIOUR.

S. Jesus said, I am the bread of life; he that cometh to me shall never hunger, and he that believeth on me shall never thirst.

P. The bread of God is he who cometh down and giveth life unto the world.

S. To this end was I born, and for this cause came I into the world, that I should bear witness unto the truth.

P. I am come, a light into the world, that whosoever believeth on me should not abide in darkness.

S. I am the good Shepherd, that giveth his life for the sheep.

P. I am the good Shepherd, and know my sheep, and am known of mine.

S. I am the door of the sheep. By me if any man enter in, he shall be saved;

P. And shall go in and out, and find pasture.

S. I am the vine, ye are the branches. He that abideth in me, and I in him, the same bringeth forth much fruit; for without me ye can do nothing.

P. As the branch cannot bear fruit except it abide in the vine, no more can ye except ye abide in me.

S. If ye keep my commandments, ye shall abide in my love, even as I have kept my Father's commandments, and abide in his love.

P. This is my commandment, that ye love one another, as I have loved you.

S. Greater love hath no man than this, that a man lay down his life for his friend.

P. Ye are my friends, if ye do whatsoever I command you.

S. For God so loved the world, that he gave his only begotten Son, that whosoever believeth in him should not perish, but have everlasting life.

P. For God sent not his Son into the world to condemn the world, but that the world through him might be saved.

S. He whom God hath sent speaketh the

words of God; for God giveth not the Spirit by measure unto him.

P. The Father loveth the Son, and hath given all things into his hands.

S. This is a faithful saying, and worthy of all acceptation, that Jesus Christ came into the world to save sinners.

P. God having raised up his Son Jesus, sent him to bless us in turning away every one of us from his sins.

S. Blessed be the Lord God of Israel, for he hath visited and redeemed his people; and hath raised up a horn of salvation for us, in the house of his servant David.

P. As he spake by the mouth of his holy prophets, which have been since the world began.

S. To give knowledge of salvation unto his people, by the remission of their sins, through the tender mercy of our God, whereby the day-spring from on high hath visited us.

P. To give light to them that sit in darkness and in the shadow of death; to guide our feet into the way of peace.

LESSON XXXV.

PROMISES OF THE GOSPEL.

S. Blessed are the poor in spirit;
P. For theirs is the kingdom of heaven.
S. Blessed are they that mourn;
P. For they shall be comforted.
S. Blessed are the meek;
P. For they shall inherit the earth.
S. Blessed are they which do hunger and thirst after righteousness;
P. For they shall be filled.
S. Blessed are the merciful;
P. For they shall obtain mercy.
S. Blessed are the pure in heart;
P. For they shall see God.
S. Blessed are the peacemakers;
P. For they shall be called the children of God.
S. Whosoever shall confess me before men, him will I confess before my Father in heaven;

P. But whosoever shall deny me before men, him will I also deny before my Father who is in heaven.

S. My sheep hear my voice and follow me, and I will give them eternal life; and they shall never perish, neither shall any man pluck them out of my hand.

P. My Father which gave them me is greater than all, and no man is able to pluck them out of my Father's hand.

S. I will pray the Father, and he shall give you another Comforter;

P. Even the Spirit of truth, that he may abide with you for ever.

S. Peace I leave with you; my peace I give unto you.

P. Not as the world giveth, give I unto you.

S. Verily, verily I say unto you, If a man keep my saying, he shall never taste of death.

P. Whosoever liveth and believeth on me shall never die.

S. In my Father's house are many mansions. I go to prepare a place for you.

P. And if I go and prepare a place for you,

I will come again and receive you unto myself, that where I am, there ye may be also.

S. The hour is coming in the which all that are in their graves shall hear the voice of the Son of Man, and shall come forth:

P. They that have done good, unto the resurrection of life; and they that have done evil, unto the resurrection of condemnation.

S. When the Son of Man shall come in his glory, and all the holy angels with him, then shall he sit upon the throne of his glory, and before him shall be gathered all nations;

P. And he shall separate them from one another, as a shepherd divideth his sheep from the goats.

S. Then shall the king say unto them on his right hand,

P. Come, ye blessed of my Father, inherit the kingdom prepared for you from the foundation of the world.

LESSON XXXVI.

CHRISTIAN DISPOSITIONS.

S. If thou bring thy gift to the altar, and there rememberest that thy brother hath aught against thee, leave there thy gift before the altar, and go thy way; first be reconciled to thy brother, and then come and offer thy gift.

P. Mercy is better than sacrifice; and to love our neighbor as ourself is more than all whole burnt-offerings and sacrifices.

S. I say unto you, Love your enemies, bless them that curse you, do good to them that hate you, and pray for them which despitefully use you and persecute you:

P. That ye may be the children of your Father in heaven; for he maketh his sun to rise on the evil and on the good, and sendeth rain on the just and on the unjust.

S. Not every one that saith unto me, Lord,

Lord, shall enter into the kingdom of heaven; but he that doeth the will of my Father which is in heaven.

P. Whosoever shall do the will of my Father which is in heaven, the same is my brother, and sister, and mother.

S. If any man will come after me, let him deny himself, and take up his cross and follow me;

P. For whosoever will save his life shall lose it; but whosoever shall lose his life for my sake, the same shall save it.

S. What shall it profit a man if he gain the whole world, and lose his own soul?

P. What shall a man give in exchange for his soul?

S. If any man desire to be first, let him be last of all, and servant of all;

P. Even as the Son of Man came not to be ministered unto, but to minister.

S. Whosoever shall receive a little child in my name, receiveth me;

P. And whosoever receiveth me, receiveth Him that sent me.

S. There is no man that hath left house, or brethren, or sisters, or father, or mother, or wife, or children, or lands, for my sake and the gospel's, but he shall receive an hundred-fold now in this time;

P. And in the world to come, life everlasting.

S. Provide for yourselves treasures in the heavens, where no thief approacheth, neither moth corrupteth;

P. For where your treasure is, there will your heart be also.

S. Whosoever drinketh of the water that I shall give him, shall never thirst;

P. But the water that I shall give him shall be in him a well of water springing up to everlasting life.

LESSON XXXVII.

ON THE DEATH OF A YOUNG CHILD.

S. Come unto me all ye that labor and are heavy laden, and I will give you rest. Take my yoke upon you, and learn of me; for I am meek and lowly in heart, and ye shall find rest unto your souls:

P. For my yoke is easy, and my burden is light.

S. Beloved, think it not strange concerning the fiery trial which is to try you, as though some strange thing had happened unto you;

P. But rejoice, inasmuch as ye are partakers of Christ's sufferings.

S. Remember now thy Creator in the days of thy youth, while the evil days come not, nor the years draw nigh when thou shalt say, I have no pleasure in them.

P. Then shall the dust return to the earth

as it was, and the spirit shall return unto God who gave it.

S. Then were brought unto him little children, that he should put his hands on them, and pray ; and the disciples rebuked them.

P. But Jesus said, Suffer little children to come unto me, and forbid them not, for of such is the kingdom of heaven. And he took them up in his arms and blessed them.

S. Take heed, that ye despise not one of these little ones;

P. For I say unto you, that in heaven their angels do always behold the face of my Father who is in heaven.

S. Is it well with the child?

P. It is well.

S. Be ye therefore followers of God as dear children.

P. Obey your parents in all things; for this is well pleasing unto the Lord.

S. For the eyes of the Lord are over the righteous, and his ears are open to their prayers;

P. And they shall be mine, saith the Lord

of hosts, in the day when I make up my jewels.

S. Peace I leave with you; my peace I give unto you.

P. In my Father's house are many mansions. The small and the great are there. And God shall wipe away all tears from their eyes.

LESSON XXXVIII.

ON THE DEATH OF A TEACHER OR ELDER SCHOLAR.

S. My son, despise not thou the chastening of the Lord, nor faint when thou art rebuked of him;

P. For whom the Lord loveth he chasteneth, and scourgeth every son whom he receiveth.

S. Our light affliction, which is but for a moment, worketh out for us a far more exceeding and eternal weight of glory.

P. While we look not at the things which are seen, but at the things which are not seen;

S. For the things which are seen are temporal, but the things which are not seen are eternal.

P. I reckon that the sufferings of this present time are not worthy to be compared with the glory which shall be revealed in us.

S. For I am persuaded that neither life nor death; nor angels, nor principalities, nor powers; nor things present, nor things to come;

P. Nor height, nor depth, nor any other creature, shall be able to separate us from the love of God, which is in Christ Jesus our Lord.

S. I am the Resurrection and the Life:

P. He that believeth in me, though he were dead, yet shall he live; and whosoever liveth and believeth in me, shall never die.

S. In my Father's house are many mansions; if it were not so, I would have told you: I go to prepare a place for you;

P. And if I go to prepare a place for you, I will come again, and receive you unto myself, that where I am there ye may be also.

S. Behold, the tabernacle of God is with men;

P. And he will wipe away all tears from their eyes, and there shall be no more death, neither sorrow nor crying, neither shall there be any more pain.

S. This corruptible must put on incorruption, and this mortal, immortality:

P. Then shall be brought to pass this saying that is written, Death is swallowed up in victory.

S. O Death, where is thy sting?

P. O Grave, where is thy victory?

S. Thanks be to God, which giveth us the victory,

P. Through Jesus Christ our Lord.

LESSON XXXIX.

FOR A RURAL CELEBRATION.

S. The heavens declare the glory of God; and the firmament showeth his handiwork.

P. Day unto day uttereth speech, and night unto night showeth knowledge.

S. The day is thine, O God; the night also is thine.

P. Thou makest the outgoings of the morning and evening to rejoice.

S. The eyes of all wait upon thee, and thou givest them their meat in due season.

P. Thou satisfiest the desire of every living thing.

S. Thou hast established the borders of the earth; thou hast made winter and summer.

P. While the earth remaineth, seed-time and harvest, and cold and heat, and summer and winter, and day and night, shall not cease.

S. Thou crownest the year with thy goodness, and thy paths drop fatness.

P. They drop upon the pastures of the wilderness, and the little hills rejoice on every side.

S. The pastures are clothed with flocks; the valleys also are covered over with corn.

P. They shout for joy; they also sing.

S. Thou visitest the earth and waterest it.

P. Thou makest it soft with showers; thou blessest the springing thereof.

S. Behold, the sons of men go forth to their labor, and the field yieldeth food for them and their children.

P. They reap every one his corn from the field; they gather every one his vintage from the vineyard.

S. Behold the fowls of the air: for they sow not, neither do they reap; yet your Heavenly Father feedeth them.

P. He giveth to the beast his food, and to the young ravens which cry.

S. He causeth the grass to grow for the cattle, and herb for the service of man.

P. He sendeth the springs into the valleys, which run among the hills.

S. The mountains and the hills break forth into singing;

P. And all the trees of the field clap their hands.

S. O Lord, how manifold are thy works! in wisdom hast thou made them all.

P. Who coverest thyself with light as with a garment; who stretchest out the heavens like a curtain.

S. The earth is full of the goodness of the Lord;

P. And his tender mercies are over all his works.

S. Bless the Lord, O our souls! and all that is within us bless his holy name.

P. We will bless thee, O Lord, as long as we live; we will give praises unto our God while we have any being.

LESSON XL.

FOR AN ANNIVERSARY CELEBRATION.

S. Lord, thou hast been our dwelling-place in all generations.

P. From everlasting to everlasting, thou art God.

S. A thousand years in thy sight are but as yesterday when it is past.

P. We spend our years as a tale that is told.

S. Thou hast determined the times before appointed, and the bounds of our habitation.

P. All our times are in thy hand.

S. We have loved the habitation of thy house, and the place where thine honor dwelleth.

P. A day in thy courts is better than a thousand.

S. One thing have we desired of the Lord, that we may dwell in the house of the Lord all the days of our lives;

P. To behold the beauty of the Lord, and to inquire in his temple.

S. Teach us thy ways, O Lord; show us thy paths.

P. Help us to walk in the way of thy commandments.

S. Blessed are they that hear the word of God, and keep it.

P. Blessed is the man whose God is the Lord.

S. Suffer the little children to come unto me, said the Saviour, for of such is the kingdom of Heaven.

P. Whosoever shall not receive the kingdom of God as a little child, shall not enter therein.

S. The Lord is nigh unto all them that call upon him.

P. His tender mercies are over all his works.

S. Let us rejoice in the Lord who hath made us.

P. Let us be joyful in God our King.

S. We will come into his presence with thanksgiving.

P. We will declare his praise among the congregation.

S. O that men would praise the Lord, for his wonderful works to the children of men!

P. For the Lord is good, his mercy is everlasting, and his truth endureth to all generations.

S. Praise ye the Lord, both young men and maidens, old men and children;

P. Let everything that hath breath praise the Lord:

S. For he hath raised up his son Jesus to be a Saviour for us;

P. To turn our footsteps from the path of evil, and reconcile our souls to God.

S. We will trust in the Lord with all our hearts;

P. And love him with all our strength.

S. May the word of Christ dwell in us richly in all wisdom;

P. And the peace of God, which passeth understanding, rule in all our hearts, henceforth and for ever.

LESSON XLI.

FOR CHRISTMAS.

S. And Joseph went up from Galilee, out of the city of Nazareth, into Judæa, unto the city of David, which is called Bethlehem, with Mary his espoused wife.

P. And she there brought forth her firstborn son, and wrapped him in swaddling-clothes, and laid him in a manger, because there was no room for them in the inn.

S. And there were in the same country shepherds abiding in the field, keeping watch over their flock by night;

P. And lo! the angel of the Lord came upon them, and the glory of the Lord shone round about them, and they were sore afraid.

S. And the angel said unto them, Fear not; for behold I bring you good tidings of great joy, which shall be to all people;

P. For unto you is born this day, in the city of David, a Saviour, who is Christ the Lord.

S. And this shall be a sign unto you: ye shall find the babe wrapped in swaddling-clothes, lying in a manger. And suddenly there was with the angel a multitude of the heavenly host, praising God and saying,

P. Glory to God in the highest, and on earth peace, good-will toward men!

S. Now, when Jesus was born in Bethlehem of Judæa, in the days of Herod the king, behold there came wise men from the east to Jerusalem, saying:

P. Where is he that is born King of the Jews; for we have seen his star in the east, and are come to worship him?

S. And Herod gathered all the chief priests and scribes of the people together, and demanded of them where Christ should be born;

P. And they said unto him, In Bethlehem of Judæa; for thus it is written by the Prophet, And thou, Bethlehem, art not the least among the princes of Judah, for out of thee shall come a Governor, that shall rule my people Israel.

S. And when the wise men departed, lo! the star which they saw in the east went before them, till it came and stood over where the young child was. And when they saw the star, they rejoiced with exceeding great joy;

P. And they opened their treasures, and presented unto him gifts, gold and frankincense and myrrh.

S. And when the parents brought the child Jesus into the temple, a just and devout man named Simeon took him in his arms, and said:

P. Lord, now lettest thou thy servant depart in peace, according to thy word;

S. For mine eyes have seen the salvation which thou hast prepared before the face of all thy people:

P. A light to lighten the Gentiles, and the glory of thy people Israel.

LESSON XLII.

CLOSE OF THE YEAR.

S. Lord, thou hast been our dwelling-place in all generations. Before the mountains were brought forth, or ever thou hadst formed the earth and the world, even from everlasting to everlasting, thou art God.

P. For a thousand years in thy sight are but as yesterday when it is past, and as a watch in the night.

S. The days of our years are threescore years and ten; and if by reason of strength they be fourscore years, yet is their strength labor and sorrow, for it is soon cut off, and we fly away.

P. So teach us to number our days, that we may apply our hearts unto wisdom.

S. Lord, make me to know mine end, and the measure of my days, that I may know how frail I am.

P. Hear my prayer, O God, and give ear

unto my cry; for I am a stranger with thee, and a sojourner, as all my fathers were.

S. What man is he that liveth and shall not see death? Shall he deliver his soul from the hand of the grave?

P. He knoweth our frame, he remembereth that we are dust.

S. As for man, his days are as grass; as a flower of the field, so he flourisheth; for the wind passeth over it, and it is gone, and the place thereof shall know it no more.

P. But the mercy of the Lord is from everlasting to everlasting upon them that fear him, and his righteousness unto children's children.

S. I will remember thy works; surely I will remember thy wonders of old.

P. I will meditate also of all thy works, and talk of thy doings.

S. Thou makest the outgoings of the morning and the evening to rejoice. Thou visitest the earth, and greatly enrichest it with the river of God, which is full of water.

P. Thou crownest the year with thy goodness, and thy paths drop fatness.

S. I will sing unto the Lord as long as I live; I will sing praise to my God while I have my being.

P. My meditation of him shall be sweet; I will be glad in the Lord.

S. O that men would praise the Lord for his goodness, and for his wonderful works to the children of men!

P. For his merciful kindness is great towards us; and the truth of the Lord endureth for ever.

LESSON XLIII.

NEW YEAR.

S. Except the Lord build the house, they labor in vain that build it.

P. Except the Lord keep the city, the watchman waketh but in vain.

S. Go to now, ye that say, To-day or to-morrow we will go into such a city, and continue there a year, and buy, and sell, and get gain. Whereas, ye know not what shall be on the morrow. For what is your life?

P. It is even a vapor, that appeareth for a little time, and then vanisheth away.

S. I will lift up mine eyes unto the hills, from whence cometh my help.

P. My help cometh from the Lord, who made heaven and earth.

S. He will not suffer thy foot to be moved. He that keepeth thee will not slumber.

P. Behold, he that keepeth Israel shall neither slumber nor sleep.

S. The Lord is thy keeper. The sun shall not smite thee by day nor the moon by night.

P. The Lord shall preserve thy going out and thy coming in from this time forth, and even for evermore.

S. I will say of the Lord, He is my refuge and my fortress, my God, in him will I trust.

P. He shall cover thee with his feathers, and under his wings shalt thou trust; his truth shall be thy shield and buckler.

S. Because thou hast made the Lord which is my refuge, even the Most High, thy habitation;

P. There shall no evil befall thee, neither shall any plague come nigh thy dwelling.

S. Some trust in chariots, and some in horses;

P. But we will remember the name of the Lord our God.

S. Watch, for ye know not what hour your Lord doth come.

P. Therefore, be ye ready; for in such an hour as ye think not the Son of Man cometh.

S. But of the times and season, brethren, ye have no need that I write unto you.

P. For yourselves know perfectly that the day of the Lord so cometh as a thief in the night.

S. But ye, brethren, are not in darkness, that that day should overtake you as a thief.

P. Therefore let us watch and be sober, putting on the breastplate of faith and love, and for an helmet the hope of salvation.

S. For God hath not appointed us to wrath, but to obtain salvation by our Lord Jesus Christ.

P. Who died for us, that whether we wake or sleep we should live together with him.

PRAYERS.

I.

FOR THE TRUE SPIRIT OF WORSHIP.

Almighty God! Father of all spirits!
Thou needest nothing of men's hands,
Seeing thou givest life and breath to all.
We rejoice that, as we need so much from thee,
From a lowly heart thou wilt not turn away.
While, at this holy hour, we bow before thee,
May thy presence be felt by our souls.
May our hearts say, God is in this place.
Open the eyes of our minds, that we may see thee.
Open our hearts, that thy love may enter.
Come and make thy dwelling within us;
Nourish us with rich and heavenly thoughts;
Fill us with gentle and sweet affections:
May our worship be in spirit and in truth.
O Thou, who art the Giver of all good,

In thanks beyond what words can utter
Would we pour out our souls before thee.
The homes sheltered by thy wings,
The ties that bind us to dear friends,
The fair world thy hand hath made,
A soul of more value than the whole world,
Jesus, the Helper and Saviour of souls, —
Father, these are thy gifts.
Take what thy children now bring to thee, —
The offering of gratitude, and love, and trust.

Nor let our worship cease with words:
May our whole life be a thank-offering;
May our cheerful duty be to thee as sacrifice;
May submission and trust rise to thee as praise·
And when the service of life is ended,
May we give thee diviner worship in heaven.
Amen.

II.

THAT WE MAY SEE GOD IN HIS WORKS.

Almighty God, great Creator of all,
Thy children bow before thy throne:
Though we see thee not with the eye,
And hear thee not with the ear,
Thou teachest us by thy spirit,
And through all thy works,
And by the life of Jesus Christ,
That thou art nigh to them that call upon thee;
That thou art the rewarder
Of all them that diligently seek thee.
May we see thee in all thy works!
The flowers of the field, the birds of heaven,
The sun, moon, and stars of the firmament, —
All are thy handiwork, and declare thee good.
The dark silence of the night,
And the bright gladness of the day,
Continually show forth thy love.

In wisdom hast thou made the world:
The earth is full of thy riches.

O God, we bless thee for thy providential love:
To thee are we indebted for our happy homes;
The counsels of a father, the smiles of a mother,
The ties of brotherly and sisterly love, —
All these are thy precious gift;
Amid our unthankfulness thou hast not forgotten us.
Thou hast borne with our sins,
And invited us to repentance;
Thou hast sent thy dearly beloved Son,
To call us home to heaven and to thee.

For all thy manifold mercies,
We would worship thee with our praises,
We would serve thee with our hearts;
And when eternity shall open to us,
May we enter thy nearer presence,
To live with thee for evermore! Amen.

III.

THANKS FOR THE ENJOYMENTS OF LIFE.

Great and good Father in heaven!
We adore thy bountiful providence.
From the stores of thy unfailing love
We see thee blessing all thy creatures:
Beast, bird, insect, all wait upon thee:
Thou openest thine hand, and they are fed.
The earth is full of thy riches.
We thank thee, that, through thy goodness,
The lines have fallen to us in pleasant places,
And we have a goodly heritage.
We thank thee for our happy homes;
For our parents, teachers, and friends;
For healthful bodies and cheerful spirits;
For the fair world in which we live;
For the innocent delights which attend our path;
For the fond hopes which invite us on;
For what past ages have given us,

Through the labors and prayers of faithful men;
For minds capable of holding communion with
thee,
Through the power of heavenly truth and love;
For souls that may attain to eternal life,
Through the grace that is in Jesus Christ.
O Blessed and Bountiful Father!
Thy gifts are more than we can number.
Our tongues shall praise thee with joyful words;
Our hearts shall love thee more than words can
tell.
All glory be to thee, the Father everlasting!
We praise thee, we worship thee;
Day by day we magnify thy holy name.
With saints and angels, we adore thee:
We thank thee that out of the mouths of children
Thou hast accepted praise.
O God! add this to thy other gifts, —
The gift of a more grateful heart.
Let thy goodness lead us to repentance:
The spirit of thine own free bounty
May we ourselves show to others.
Save us from all selfish thoughts:

Give us enlarged and generous affections:
Let the love of God be diffused through the world,
And peace and joy fill the whole earth.
And to thee, through Jesus, shall be the glory.
Amen.

IV.

THANKS FOR THE SAVIOUR.

Almighty God, who art light and love,
Who dwellest in light continually,
We adore thee, that in thy fatherly goodness
Thou hast looked down upon our sins and weakness,
And hast sent to us Jesus Christ,
To be our Teacher, Lord, and Saviour.
We desire to utter our thanks to thee
For the innocence of his childhood;
For his obedience to his parents;
For his devotion to thee through all his years.
We thank thee that he pitied the poor;
That he healed the lame and the blind;
That he relieved the sick;
That he went about doing good.
We thank thee for his compassion to the erring;
For his labors to save men from their sins:

For the excellence of his life
And the power of his death we bless thee.
For his willingness to suffer for our good,
That he even laid down his life for our sakes.
  And now we humbly beseech thee
That we may become his true disciples.
We would be lowly, gentle, obedient;
We would be truthful and faithful;
We would be willing to labor and suffer for others.
Help us, O God, in our early years
To consecrate ourselves to thee.
Give to us the grace of our Lord Jesus Christ,
That, when this mortal life is ended,
We shall be received to the presence of our Saviour,
And to thine eternal favor. Amen.

V.

THANKS FOR CHRISTIAN PRIVILEGES.

We bow before thee, Almighty Father,
With our lowly but hearty thanks;
For all the blessings of our earthly lot;
Especially for this unspeakable gift,
That our birth was in a Christian land.
O God, blessed be thy holy name,
That thou didst send the Sun of Righteousness,
With healing in his beams.
Thanks for the new morn that hath risen on the world;
For the justice and right which guard the state;
For the purity and peace which bless our homes.
Thanks for thy Sabbath, — type of heavenly rest;
Thanks for the Gospel, — bread of eternal life;
Thanks for that new interest in childhood
Awakened by Him who turned the hearts
Of children to their parents,

And of parents to their children ;
Thanks for the new meaning to life
Given by Him who revealed life's end ;
Thanks for that life and immortality
Which are brought to light in the Gospel.
O Father, these blessings we owe
To thy rich love in Jesus Christ.
We praise thee for him, the Saviour of souls ;
We thank thee that we may call him dear and precious.
May we love him as coming from the bosom of the Father ;
May we give to him our young and fresh hearts ;
May he have heathen lands for his inheritance,
The uttermost parts of the earth for his possession,
Till all flesh shall see his salvation :
And to thy holy name be the glory. Amen.

VI.

THANKS FOR RELIGIOUS INSTRUCTION.

FATHER of all the children of men!
Though dwelling in the high and lofty place,
Thou art with them also of a lowly heart.
We thank thee that to our humble prayer
Thou wilt turn a listening ear.
Thou lovest them that love thee:
Those that seek thee early shall find thee.

We praise thee that we have been taught of God.
We thank thee that the Sabbath morning
Gathers us together in this sacred place,
With cheerful faces and joyful hearts,
Amid words of prayer and songs of praise,
To receive instruction from thy Truth,
To sit at the feet of Jesus,
To learn the way of eternal life.

O God, how good hast thou been to us,
In sending thy Son to save us;

In handing down to us thy Word of truth;
In appointing for our use this sacred day;
In providing for us pastors and teachers;
In giving us these ties of love,
That bind us to one another and to thee!
O Father, we cannot speak our thanks!
Thou knowest the feelings of our hearts.
May we prove the sincerity of our gratitude
By the use we make of thy gifts.
To us may the hours of this day be holy;
To us may thy word be precious.
Here may we listen to the voice of instruction;
Here may we feel the presence of Jesus;
And, cherishing his words and spirit in our hearts,
May we be fitted for life's coming scenes,
For duties in which we shall need thy light,
For trials in which we shall need thy strength.
O God, we cannot think of our blessings
Without remembering those who know them not.
To how many the light of this holy day
Brings none of the lessons, enjoyments, and hopes
Which make it so dear to us.
To the dark places of the earth,

To distant lands and heathen isles,
Send the light of thy glorious word.
Give us a heart to diffuse its joy.
Let the earth be filled with thy glory,
And all thy children share thy salvation.

Amen.

VII.

ON A BEAUTIFUL SUNDAY MORNING.

Great and good Father in heaven,
Thine is the beauty of this fair day.
Thy Spirit, which in the beginning
Moved on the face of thy works,
Still broods over earth, sea, and sky, —
The spirit of peace and of love.
From our happy homes we come,
Here to utter forth thy praise.
The bright light of thy sun,
The pure air we breathe,
The lilies of the field,
The birds of the air,
The order and bounty of thy universe,
All pay their silent worship.
Through us may they find a voice:
We would utter our and their praise.
With children of unnumbered Sunday schools,

With gathered multitudes in all lands,
Encompassing the world with anthems of joy,
Would we bring our young voices and glad hearts.
Father, thou hast made this world beautiful;
But thou hast a world of fairer beauty
For all them that love thee.
There is no night there;
No sickness, sorrowing, nor death.
In thy time may we there be received.
May we here cherish pure affections,
There to fill our hearts for ever;
May we here delight in thy worship,
There to be our joy for ages without end.
We ask it in the name of our dear Saviour.

Amen.

VIII.

FOR A GOOD IMPROVEMENT OF BLESSINGS.

O God, the Giver of all good!
We have nothing that is not thine.
May we look upon the blessings in our hands
As talents committed to our trust.
We pray that upon all thy gifts
We may see written thy holy will.
May the light of day call to thy service;
May night's darkness tell us of thy care;
May our strength be strength to do good;
May glad spirits be rejoicing in God;
May books and teachers prove our willingness to learn;
May time be valued as a sacred trust;
May the love we cherish for earthly friends
Lead us to thee, who art Love itself;
May the fair world in which we live
Be a prophecy of a fairer world to come.

Thus, O God, even in our early years,
May we be thoughtful, wise, and dutiful.
Save us from the haste which never thinks,
And from that mirthfulness which knows no serious
care.
Teach us by thy holy child Jesus
To be about our Father's business;
And while we rejoice in our youth,
And our hearts cheer us in the days of our youth,
May we know that for all things
God will bring us into judgment.

Father Almighty, for that solemn hour
May we, through thy grace, be prepared;
And, found faithful over a few things,
May we be rulers over many things,
To the glory of thy holy name. Amen.

IX.

FOR A RIGHT TEMPER.

ALMIGHTY and ever blessed God,
We worship thee, who art supremely good.
Thy dealings with us all are kind,
And thy commandments all are wise.
May we be submissive to thy will.
If our days are spent in peace,
It is because thou lovest us;
And if in trouble and in want,
Still we believe thou lovest us.
We know that when we do well,
Thou rewardest us with joy;
And when we have done evil,
Thou callest us back to goodness and to thee.
We pray thee to strengthen our hearts:
Never may we sin against thy goodness.
May we be kind to one another,
Obedient to our parents,

Respectful to the aged and the wise,
Compassionate to the suffering,
Showing honor even to the humblest:
May we be peaceful, meek, and gentle.
Fill thou our hearts with love;
May the God of peace and love dwell with us.
And when, at last, we pass the hour of death,
May we be received to Christ our Redeemer,
To the companionship of the good,
And to thine ever-blessed service. Amen.

X.

FOR GENTLENESS AND KINDNESS.

O Holy Father! Eternal God!
We thy children bow before thee;
Up to thy throne would we lift
The prayer of our youthful hearts.
We come to ask of thee, O God,
That wisdom which is pure and gentle:
We implore that fruit of the Spirit
Which is gentleness and goodness.
Help us to have control over ourselves;
Help us to put on meekness and gentleness.
In the animation of youthful spirits,
In our intercourse with our parents and friends,
In calls to resign our favorite plans,
In the provocations of impatience and anger,
May we learn the gentleness of Christ,
And be ourselves clothed with his heavenly spiri

12*

Father, we would not trust ourselves.
We remember that we have been hasty and rash:
Forgive this sin, and all our offences.
For our help we fly to thee;
Let thoughts of thy presence restrain us;
May the gentle and meek Jesus help us.
O that kindness and love may rule in our hearts!
Give us, amid the strifes of a rude world,
The gentle spirit that overcomes the mighty,
The gentle words that turn away wrath.
O Father, our Lord and God for ever!
This is the spirit in which we would live;
In this spirit would we die.
And wilt thou, the God of gentleness and love,
In thy time, take us to live with thee. Amen.

XI.

FOR LOVE TO ALL.

O Thou who art the great Creator
And sovereign Ruler over all worlds,
When we worship before thy throne,
We thank thee that we may call thee Father.
In thy presence we live,
And by thy kindness we are supported.
Thou doest all things well;
Thou lovest all whom thou hast created.
The beams of thy sun visit the just and the unjust;
Thy showers fall on the thankful and the unthankful.
In the fulness of thy mercy,
Thou art good, even to the poorest sinner
Who forgets thy holy name.
We pray that, like thee, Heavenly Father,
We may love all the members of thy family.
Give us hearts to compassionate the suffering,

To relieve the poor,
To care for the sick,
To befriend the friendless,
To do good as we have opportunity to all.
Give warmth to our sympathy,
And tenderness to our love.
We pray to thee, Heavenly Father,
For the redemption of all mankind
From sin and sorrow ;
For the growth of all in purity and kindness,
And that they may obtain thine acceptance in heaven.

We thank thee that in thy dear Son
We have an example of all generous affections ;
That he came to seek and to save the lost,
That to every form of suffering he ministered.
May his blessed spirit rule in our hearts,
And his kingdom of love be established within us.
To thy name, through him, be the glory. Amen.

XII.

FOR UNFAILING LOVE.

Our Father who art in heaven,
We acknowledge thee the best of beings.
All this great world around us, —
The far-shining stars of night,
The fields, the rivers, the mountains, —
All were made by thy wisdom and thy goodness.
The countless generations of mankind
Were formed by thee in love.
Thy dealings have been ever good,
And thy commandments all are just.

O God, help us in our weakness,
That we may love thee as we ought.
May we love thee in our prayers;
May we love thee in our labors;
May we love thee in our recreations;
When we are at home,
And when we are abroad;

When we are in society,
And when we are alone;
In the silence of the night,
Amid the cares of the day,
Still may our hearts be moved by love to thee.
Bless us, O God, through thine almighty power,
Through thine infinite wisdom;
By that Saviour whom thou didst send to us;
With that Holy Spirit that still comes from thee;
Bless us in the enjoyments of life;
Bless us in the hour of death;
Through all the scenes of time,
And through the ages of eternity;
And to thy great name be everlasting praises.

Amen.

XIII.

FOR A CHILDHOOD LIKE THAT OF JESUS.

God and Father of Jesus Christ!
Whom he worshipped with praise and prayer;
To whom he has directed us to go,
Telling us that him thou always hearest,
And whatsoever we ask in his name,
Thou wilt give it to us.

May we be like thy beloved Son:
Bearing his image in every period of life,
May we bear it especially in our early years.
Like him, in the spirit of gentle obedience,
May we be subject to our parents;
Like him, as we increase in stature,
May we grow in favor with God and man;
Like him, may we love thy holy house,
And seek the teachers of heavenly truth;
Like him, may we feel our tie to thee,
And be about our Father's business;

Like him, may we take up life's work,
Giving ourselves wholly to thy service,
With a meek and lowly temper,
Willing to suffer, patient to bear;
Remembering that for this we are born,
And for this purpose are sent into the world,
That we may bear witness to the truth.

Holy Father, thus do we pray to thee,
We, who are so far behind Him,
Who, though tempted, yet knew no sin.
To the heights of his spotless purity
We would lift up adoring eyes.
May something of the grace of that holy child
Rest on us, thy children, now:
And to thee, through him, be the glory. Amen.

XIV.

FOR AN EARLY CONSECRATION TO CHRIST.

O Father of our Lord and Christ!
Who hast given us thy holy child Jesus,
A new and living Way to thee,
A pattern in duty, a guide to truth,
A Saviour of all that call on his name;
We thank thee for this unspeakable gift.
For ever blessed be the Lord our God,
That on us this light hath arisen,
That to us this salvation hath come.

Impress upon our minds, we pray thee,
That we are sharers of this great blessing,
Not by flesh, nor by the will of man,
Only by Christ's spirit in our hearts.
To him, our rightful Lord and Master,
Would we now give ourselves;
To him, the Shepherd of Souls,
We come as lambs of his flock;

To him, the only name given under heaven
Whereby we can be saved from our sins,
Would we look, with believing and grateful hearts,
For pardon and eternal life.
O God, his God and Father, and ours,
Bless this purpose of our souls;
Help us to arise and follow Jesus;
In his footsteps may we daily walk;
His be the temper of our inmost hearts.
Thus joined to Christ on earth,
May we be gathered into his fold in heaven,
And neither life nor death separate us
From the love of God in Jesus Christ.
To thy holy name be the glory for ever. Amen.

XV.

TO BE IN THE FOLD OF THE GOOD SHEPHERD.

O Thou who sent thy Son into the world
To gather a company unto himself,
We thank thee that, through thy help,
He established his Church among men;
We thank thee that it endures to this day,—
For the multitudes of believers it has enrolled,
For its holy and beautiful rites,
For the pure faith it has nourished,
For the devout love it has sheltered,
For the noble works it has inspired;
We thank thee that its precious promise
Is to believers and their children,
And that even we in our youth
May be lambs of the Good Shepherd's flock.
O God, may we rejoice to be members
In that protected and blessed fold;
May we follow the voice of the Shepherd;

May his arms of love encircle us;
May the washing of thy pure spirit,
Set forth by the water of baptism,
Make our hearts clean in thy sight;
And while the dew of our youth is on us,
May we reverence the table of Jesus,
And eat and drink in his remembrance;
By life and conversation may we give proof
That we have been with Jesus,
And by sweet affections and holy deeds
Show that we have learned of him.
Father Almighty, thus joined to Christ on earth,
May we be of his Church in heaven,
With saints of all ages and thy holy angels,
Through Him who loved us and gave himself for us.
Amen.

XVI.

FOR A SENSE OF DEPENDENCE ON GOD.

O LORD, our Heavenly Father,
We humbly bow before thy throne;
We acknowledge and we worship thee;
We thank thee that we are the children of thy love;
Thou hast made us, and not we ourselves;
Thou watchest over us by night;
Thou keepest all our steps by day;
We can never go from thy presence,
Nor flee from thy spirit;
Thou art holy and thou art wise;
Thy commandments are good;
Thy tender mercies are over all thy works.
O God, bless us, thy lowly children;
Teach us thy holy will;
May we rely on thy providence and bounty;
Forgive the sins of which we have been guilty,
And, because we are weak in ourselves,

May we find our strength in God;
Give us, in this world, peace and joy;
And, since thou art Lord of heaven and earth,
And after death wilt raise us to another life,
We pray thee mercifully to receive us hereafter,
And give us a place among thy blessed angels,
Where we may for ever serve and love thee.
We offer our prayers to thee in the name of Jesus,
Who has taught us of the Fatherly care
Which numbers the hairs of our head,
And without which not a sparrow falleth to the ground:
On this in life and death we would depend.
Through him to thee be glory for ever. Amen.

XVII.

FOR STRENGTH IN TEMPTATION.

O God, who hast revealed thyself to us
As merciful, tender, and full of compassion,
Have pity upon us in our weakness,
And give us victory over our temptations.
We see that we often do that which is wrong:
Thine eye sees failings to which we are blind.
O God, feeble, wandering, and falling,
We come to thee for help.
All-knowing Father, teach us to know ourselves;
Reveal to us the true source of our failings;
Make us feel that our sins cleave to us,
Because we have not thy spirit within;
Teach us to lean, not on ourselves, but on thee;
Give us thy strength perfect in our weakness;
Create in us a clean heart,
Renew a right spirit within us;
Show us how we can do all things,

Through Him who strengtheneth us,
And who, himself tempted as we are,
Was yet without sin.
Let the faith that was in him
Be our shield to quench the darts of evil;
May we stand with our feet shod with his truth,
And our loins girt about by his word;
Amid all trials may we watch unto prayer.
O Father, our refuge, our strength, our rock,
Hear us, thy frail and tempted children;
And let the struggles and perils of this life
Fit us for a world of peace and blessedness,
To which in thy time may we be received,
Through thy merciful kindness in Jesus Christ.
Amen.

XVIII.

FOR GOOD THOUGHTS.

O God, our great Creator,
We adore thee, and we thank thee
That thou hast made man a living soul;
We thank thee that the thoughts of our minds
And the love within our hearts
May live through everlasting ages.
We would remember that thou searchest us,
To see if there be any wicked way in us.
Aid us by thy Spirit perfect in our weakness,
That our hearts may be wholly pure.
And since at times our thoughts mislead us,
And we are betrayed into evil ere we are aware,
We pray that thou wouldst guide our thoughts,
And make them acceptable to thee.
May there be no proud thoughts within us;
May angry thoughts be put far from us;
Save us from envious and selfish thoughts;

Give us thoughts humble before thee,
Reverent for thy truth,
Gentle towards our equals,
Obedient to our parents
And to all who are set over us by thee;
Help us to possess in our souls
The loveliness of the spirit of Jesus,
His purity, simplicity, and sincerity;
Breathe holy desires into our hearts;
Let good thoughts come like good angels to our minds;
May we be obedient to the heavenly vision,
And let them not go till they have blessed us.
Thus may we love thee while we live on earth,
And hereafter enter the nearer presence
Of thy perfect love in heaven. Amen.

XIX.

FOR FAITHFULNESS IN DUTY.

Our Father, who art in heaven,
With the voice of prayer we seek thee;
Encouraged by the promise of thy Word,
That thou art more ready than our earthly parents
To give thy best gifts unto us.
We thank thee, that thou, our Master,
Hast assigned work to all thy children;
And that something, in thy service,
Even such as we can do;
We know that we may have thy favor,
If only we do what we can;
May pure motives and sweet affections
Guide and beautify our lives;
In our studies may we be diligent;
May our recreations be always innocent;
To our teachers may we be attentive;
May our relation to parents, brothers, and sisters

Be marked by respect, kindness, and love;
May we bear our little trials with patience;
May we yield our preferences with cheerfulness;
May we not selfishly seek our own pleasure,
But study to promote the enjoyment of others;
If we are ever betrayed into anger,
Help us to restrain our feelings,
And to put far from us all strife;
Never may we darken our homes
By a disobedient and sullen spirit;
But may our presence give the light
Of generous feelings and cheerful hearts;
And when at night we seek our pillow,
And offer to thee our evening prayer,
May we be able to recall something we have done
To make the day useful and happy.
O God, may this spirit mark our early years,
And grow with our growth while we live;
May a life of usefulness and happiness on earth
Fit us for the service and joy of heaven,
Through thy grace in the Redeemer of Souls.
Amen.

XX.

THAT WE MAY FOLLOW THE EXAMPLE OF GOOD MEN.

Father of our Lord Jesus Christ,
Whom thou didst send into the world
To be our perfect example in duty,
We thank thee that the lives of the good
Animate and quicken our hearts,
And plead with us to walk in their steps;
May this response to a noble example
Be as the voice of God in the soul.

We thank thee that there have been those
Whose lives shine as the light, —
Holy men who have feared God,
Brave men who have upheld the right,
Generous men who have lived for others' good,
Men who chose suffering rather than wrong,
And felt thy favor to be better than life.

Our Father in heaven, we thank thee,

That, without the honors and riches of this world,
Verily they have their reward,
In the approval of their consciences
And in the smiles of thy love.
We mark the perfect man and upright,
For the end of that man is peace.
O let their pure and noble lives
Be a trumpet-call to our hearts;
May we feel that in our humble sphere
We may exercise their faith, their courage,
Their love for man, their fear of God;
Above all, draw us to Him
In whom centre all rays of excellence;
And in our souls may there burn a desire
To be like thy Son Jesus Christ. Amen.

XXI.

TO BE GUIDED INTO ALL TRUTH.

Almighty God, who art light,
And with whom there is no darkness,
To thee thy children now come,
That in thy light we may see light.
Mercifully hear our lowly prayer,
And give us the wisdom that is from above.
Save us from all that would blind our minds,
From pride, presumption, and self-will,
From contentment with imperfect views,
From neglect of continued study of thy Word.
May our hearts be open as the day,
May they long for more quickening truth.
As we sit at the feet of Jesus,
On us be the blessings he pronounced
On the poor in spirit and the pure in heart.
Give us clear views of thy Word, —
The truth that is not a spirit of bondage to fear,

But of love and of a sound mind;
The truth that sanctifieth and maketh free;
That binds us to Jesus and allies us to God;
That ennobles life and is victorious over death.
  While we love what to us thou teachest,
And cling to it as the anchor of our souls,
May we remember our Master has other servants;
That to him alone they stand or fall.
Give us love for all who love thee.
Amid diversities of belief,
May there be the spirit of truth, —
The unity of the spirit in the bond of peace.
  O God, send forth thy truth and light:
Over error and wrong and sin be it triumphant,
Till all know thee, the only true God,
And Jesus Christ whom thou hast sent. Amen.

XXII.

FOR OUR HOMES.

OUR Father who art in heaven,
We thank thee that we know thy name;
And we bow down and worship thee,
Father of all the families of earth.
We thank thee for our homes,
For a father's and a mother's love,
And for all the kindness shown to us.
We pray that, as sons and daughters,
We may be faithful to our parents,
And may always truly love them.
If we have been secretly disobedient to them,
Or have openly sinned against them,
Before the face of thine exalted purity
We humbly confess our sin,
And implore thy divine forgiveness.
And now, so may we live, O God,
That father and mother, and brother and sister,

And all whom we ought to love,
By our kind deeds and gentle words
May be made happy every day.
Save us from being selfish, thoughtless, and unjust:
May our temper be meek, gentle, affectionate;
And, when we have done all that we can
To make our homes happy upon earth,
May we be received, at last, with all we love,
To the mansions of the home in heaven.

For the hope of that heavenly home,
For the memory of loved ones there gathered,
For the welcome they may give to us,
For the guidance of the Shepherd of the flock,
For the great family in heaven and on earth,
We will give thee, now and ever, our thanks.

Amen.

XXIII.

FOR THE POOR AND SUFFERING.

Almighty God, our Heavenly Father,
Who hast made of one blood all nations of men,
To dwell on the face of the earth ;
The high and the humble,
The rich and the poor, are thine:
The Lord is the maker of them all.
We thank thee for all the good things
We are ourselves permitted to enjoy:
For our comfortable and happy homes,
For kind parents, wise and faithful friends.
Help us, O God, that in our abundance
We may remember the poor and suffering:
Hear thou our prayers for their sakes;
Give to them in their needs;
Shield them in their exposures;
Bless the widow and the orphan;
Wipe away the tears from the afflicted:

What thou of thy bounty givest us
May we share with the needy.
In the friendless and the suffering,
May we see the person of Jesus;
And hear his voice say to us,
Because ye did it unto them,
Ye did it unto me.
Father, we pray that his tender spirit
May yet more and more prevail in the world,
And be triumphant over human woe.
And to thy great name, through him,
Be glory and honor for ever. Amen.

XXIV.

FOR A HOPE FULL OF IMMORTALITY.

ALMIGHTY GOD, who livest for ever,
Without beginning of years or end of days;
Though our earthly life be a span,
We have a hope of a life eternal.
Blessed be the Lord our God,
Who has begotten us to this lively hope,
By the resurrection of our Lord from the dead.
May the power of the life to come
Be felt in the life that now is.
May we see that the gain of the whole world
Shall at last profit us nothing,
If we lose our own soul;
And that nothing can be given
In exchange for the soul.
Beyond things seen and temporal
May we extend the vision of our faith,
And live for interests that shall endure
When the stars of the firmament shall perish.

May we diligently sow the seed
That shall bear fruit to eternal life;
May the thought of the world to come
Lift up and ennoble all our aims,
Giving us patience in our trials,
Making life a sacred discipline,
And death seem but as a new birth.
May we feel that friends departed in Christ
Are not lost, but are in that heavenly home
Which Jesus has gone before to prepare;
And that, one day, they will there welcome
The loved who shall follow in their steps.
O God, grant that no sins
May darken this precious hope.
Give us that divine spirit
Which abolishes all thought of death,
And fits us for the company of the pure in heart,
Who shall for ever see God.
We offer our prayer in the name of Him
Who is the resurrection and the life,
Who brought life and immortality to light,
For whose salvation we thank thee,
And through whom to thee be the praise for ever.
Amen.

XXV.

FOR A FRIEND WHO IS SICK.

Almighty God, most merciful Father,
Who sendest forth thy Spirit, and we are created;
Who hidest thy face, and we are troubled;
Who takest away our breath, and we die:
With thee are the issues of all things;
And health and sickness, life and death,
Are the messengers of thy will.
We offer our supplications unto thee
For our friend who is sick;
That this sickness may not be unto death,
But for the glory of God.
O thou, who art our life and our health,
Bless the means used for recovery;
Stay the progress of wasting disease;
Bring back strength to the feeble;
Give our friend many years to see good,
And to devote restored life to thy service.

Father, not our will, but thine, be done.
If this sickness is to be the last sickness,
And this bed to be the bed of death,
O God, prepare all hearts for thy will.
Give us the supports of submission and trust;
May we find the balm in Gilead,
And know that there is a Physician there,
Who, though the outward man perish,
Can renew the inward man day by day.
Impart that faith in the Lord Jesus Christ
Which triumphs over the decays of mortality,
And by which death is swallowed up in life.
Father, may the remembrance of our frailty
Call us to begin, without delay,
Our preparation for days of weakness and decline,
Which shall surely come to us also.
And at last, through thy grace in Jesus Christ,
Reunite us in peace, in that world
Where there is no sickness, nor sorrowing, nor death. Amen.

XXVI.

ON THE DEATH OF AN ELDER SCHOLAR, OR TEACHER.

O Lord, our Heavenly Father,
The Giver of Life, and the Disposer of Death.
Since, in thine infinite wisdom,
It hath pleased thee to remove from us our friend,
We bow with humble submission,
And adore thee, the greatest and best of beings.
Even in our tears, our prayer shall be, —
Father, not our will, but thine be done.

We thank thee for the life our friend here lived,
For the happy hours which memory brings to mind.
We bless thee that we have often been permitted
To engage in thy worship with the departed.
That voice will no more be heard by us;
That smile will no more be seen by us;
Yet thou lovest us who are still left,
And thou lovest those who have been taken:

Thou art God of the spirits of the departed,
As much as of thy children in this visible world.
Comfort us, we beseech thee, in our affliction;
And in the bereavement which we endure,
Exalt our minds, that, with a true faith,
Our hearts may follow after the absent
To the world to which they have gone.
May we receive with tender hearts
The lessons death is designed to give.
May it seem like putting off the perishable,
So that nothing but life may remain.
May it seem like a new birth,
To a world where death is unknown.
Teach us to live as those who are about to die;
Teach us to live as those who shall live for ever,
In the blessedness of thy heavenly presence,
With Christ and the holy angels,
And with all whom we have truly loved on earth.
Merciful Father, forgive our sins;
Strengthen us in all goodness,
In meekness, humility, faith, and patience.
And unto thee who lovest us,
Through Christ who died for us,
Be all praise and glory for ever. Amen.

XXVII.

ON THE DEATH OF A YOUNGER SCHOLAR.

Almighty God, we humbly adore thee:
Thou art the author and the giver of life.
We thank thee, that as in love thou dost create us,
And in love thou dost watch over and preserve us,
In equal love thou appointest the day of our death.
We bless thee for the life of the little child
Whom thy wise providence hath taken from us;
We thank thee for its innocence,
For its sweetness of temper,
And the fulness of its love.
We shall see it no more in this world,
But it dwells with thee.
We rejoice in the assurance of Jesus,
That its angel doth always behold the face
Of our Father who is in heaven.
And now help us, Almighty God,
To bear our sorrow with a cheerful trust.

Enlarge our hearts by faith,
That we may believe in the immortal world;
Prepare our souls, by all thy wise admonitions,
That we, being delivered from all sins,
And being strengthened in the love of all good,
May be worthy to enter thine eternal inheritance.
O God, we pray thee, comfort the afflicted;
Visit their hearts with peace;
Wipe the tears from their eyes;
Let thy spirit dwell in their souls with love;
Help them to serve thee truly in this world,
And receive them at last to the loved and the lost,
Where there is no more sorrowing nor death;
And to thy great name, through Jesus Christ,
The dear Redeemer who hath abolished death,
Be praises everlasting. Amen.

XXVIII.

AT AN ANNIVERSARY CELEBRATION.

ALMIGHTY GOD, our Heavenly Father,
Who hast made the heavens fair above our heads,
And the earth beautiful beneath our feet;
Who hast given health to our bodies,
And hast filled our hearts with joy;
We bow with gladness before thy throne,
To worship thee, the Infinite and Holy One.

Bless us in this day of our assembling;
Bless the friends who are with us,
And the friends we love who are absent.
Teach us thy lessons from the scene around us;
In the midst of the young and the happy,
May our hearts be pure, gentle, and devout;
May the air of heaven breathe to us its purity,
The clouds above us tell of thy goodness,
And the lofty sky lift up our souls
To the heaven in which thou dwellest.

O God, in sparing our lives to this day,
We recognize thy fatherly goodness;
We thank thee for the year that is passed,
And for all its opportunities and lessons;
Forgive our neglects and sins;
Help us to mark this day
By a renewed consecration to thee.
We bless thee for gifts prolonged by thy love;
We bless thee for hopes of greater faithfulness
To mark our future way;
We bless thee for the memory of departed friends,
And for good people of all ages;
We bless thee for Christ, the dear Redeemer,
Whose faithful disciples we pray that we may be,
And by whom may we be accepted,
When we shall be called from this present world
To thy world of unseen glory and blessedness.
Amen.

XXIX.

AT A RURAL CELEBRATION.

God of Nature, God of Grace,
Who hath made for us two great lights:
The glorious light of thy Works,
The glorious light of thy Word.
We thank thee for both of these teachers,
And that both are thy harmonious voice
To all the children of men.

While we read the page of thy elder scripture,
We bow down to worship thee.
Thine the sun, the light, the sky;
Thine the hills, the trees, the grass;
Thine the breath of flowers, the song of bird;
Thine the smile on the face of nature;
Thine this deep tide of life and joy;
Thine the fair, round world, full of thy riches:
O God, in wisdom hast thou made thy works.
For thy pleasure are they created,
To declare the invisible things of thee:

Thy Godhead, thy power, thy goodness;
To lift up all our hearts to thee
In grateful and adoring trust.
Father Almighty, to thee do we come.
Let thy majesty humble our souls;
Let thy benignity give them joy;
And while we muse on the calm silence around,
May we thank thee that to it thou hast added
A voice, sublime as the stars,
Sweet as the breath of morn,
Which speaks pardon to repented sins,
And gives the promise of eternal life.
For Jesus we will here thank thee;
For the Christian's life, and the Christian's hope.
O God, may the moments here passed
Be moments of pure and devout joy.
Let thoughts of thy presence and love
Hallow our greetings and recreations.
May we go back to life's varied work
Refreshed for more dutiful toil;
Grateful for this beautiful world;
Grateful for all kindly affections;
Grateful for the hope of reunion in heaven.
Amen.

XXX.

AT CHRISTMAS.

OUR Father in heaven, hallowed be thy name!
With the voice of praise do we come to thee,
That thou hast visited us in our low estate,
And raised up for us a Saviour,
Promised of old by thy holy Prophets,
And declared to be the Son of God with power.
Thanks that the song has encircled the earth
Which was first heard on Bethlehem's plain:
Glory to God in the highest,
Peace on earth, good-will towards men.
May our hearts be attuned to that praise,
And, from the fulness of our joy for a Saviour,
May we take up and repeat the anthem:
Glory to God in the highest!
Thanks that we may bring gifts to thy child Jesus;
That the poorest may open treasures for him.
Assurance that on him thou hast laid our help,

Hearts joyful in the truth he brings from heaven,
Souls longing to possess his divine life, —
Father, these are our offerings ; if sincere,
More precious to thy pure eyes
Than gold, frankincense, and myrrh.

O God, may every return of this day
Witness new triumphs of the kingdom of thy Son.
Give it more power in each of our souls ;
Extend its dominion of truth, peace, and love ;
Bless all efforts to send it abroad through the world,
Till the uttermost parts of the earth shall rejoice,
And all flesh shall see the salvation of God.
Amen.

XXXI.

AT THE CLOSE OF THE YEAR.

Almighty God, who inhabitest eternity,
Who art without beginning of years,
And whose days shall have no end;
We, thy children, who are of yesterday,
And whose life passes away as a tale,
Lift to thee our lowly prayer.
Ackowledging thy care, we look back
Upon the way in which thou hast led us.
Thy seasons have visited us in turn;
Thy hand hath supplied our wants;
Thy love hath bestowed our enjoyments;
Thy wisdom hath appointed our trials;
And because we have obtained help from thee,
We have continued to this time.
Bless the Lord, O my soul,
And forget not all his benefits,
Who healeth all thy sicknesses,

Who redeemeth thy life from destruction,
Who crownest thy days with goodness.
O God, with thoughtful minds may we remember
That a year of our life is gone,
Its moments never to be recalled,
Its record never to be changed.
If that record tells of our neglect,
Of our disobedience to parents,
Of our unkindness to one another,
Of our misuse of our time,
Of our forgetfulness of God,
May not the last sun of this year go down
On unrepented and unforgiven sins;
For thy mercy's sake, grant us thy pardon.
Father, in this solemn hour,
We remember those, a year since with us,
Whom we shall see on earth no more;
No more shall they join in our prayers,
No more lift their voices in our songs.
We hope their angels are around thy throne.
For their higher worship in heaven
May these fleeting years prepare us,
That we may join their company

When our days on earth are passed.
So teach us to number our days
That we may apply our hearts unto wisdom.
Father, we offer our prayer to thee,
For that spirit of Jesus which is life eternal,
Which lifts us above all changes of time,
And gives us a foretaste of immortality.
With stronger faith, and quickened diligence,
May we seek Him, the Way, the Truth, the Life;
May our life be hid in his,
And be safe and enduring for ever.
To thee be the glory, through him. Amen.

XXXII.

AT THE BEGINNING OF THE YEAR.

God of the changing seasons!
Who fulfillest to us thy promise,
That as long as the earth endures,
Summer and winter shall not fail;
Thine is the light of this new year;
We pray that it may be consecrated to thee.
Accept our thanks for this new gift.
With joy we enter on this new scene.
While for all we wish it may be happy,
Father, we feel that the fulfilment is with thee.
We know not what shall be on the morrow:
All our times are in thy hand.
To thee we bring our hopes and our plans;
O God, do with them and with us
As seemeth right in thy sight.
We pray that this year may be new,
By bringing new thoughts of God,

New longings for thy Spirit,
New resolutions for thy service.
If it be the last year we see on earth,
May it be the best of our lives;
If we live to its close, may that find us
More truly children of God.
We would not be anxious about coming days:
We leave the ordering of our lot to thee,
Feeling that we are in our Father's house,
And are safe beneath a Father's eye.
Not of thee, but of ourselves, are we distrustful.
Keep us from the neglects of former years;
Help us to be more thoughtful and diligent,
More watchful and prayerful in temptation,
More alive to the true work of life,
More strong in the spirit of our divine Master.

Standing at the opening of this new scene,
We pray for thy blessing on our friends;
Be with our parents, brothers, and sisters;
May our homes be homes of peace and love;
Bless our pastor and our teachers.
May the Sabbaths of this coming year
Give new power to thy truth and grace;

Let the Gospel of thy dear Son
Have success in its purpose of love;
And the spirit and power of his cross
Triumph over the woes of the world.
To him be glory in his Church for ever. Amen

HYMNS.

16*

HYMNS.

---

1. C. M.

1 FATHER in heaven, to whom our hearts
Would lift themselves in prayer,
Drive from our souls each earthly thought,
And show thy presence there.

2 Help us to break the galling chains
This world has round us thrown;
Each passion of our hearts subdue,
Each cherished sin disown.

3 O Father! kindle in our souls
A never-dying flame
Of holy love, of grateful trust
In thine almighty name.

2. C. M.

1 WHAT secret hand, at morning light,
Softly unseals mine eye,
Draws back the curtain of the night,
And opens earth and sky?

2 'T is thine, O God! — the same that kept
My resting hours from harm;
No ill came near me, for I slept
Beneath th' Almighty's arm.

3 May that sure hand uphold me still
Through life's uncertain race,
To bring me to thy holy hill,
And to thy dwelling-place.

3. C. M.

1 BLEST day of God! most calm, most bright,
The first and best of days;
The laborer's rest, the saint's delight,
The day of prayer and praise!

2 My Saviour's face made thee to shine
His rising thee did raise;
And made thee heavenly and divine
Beyond all other days.

3 The first-fruits oft a blessing prove
To all the sheaves behind;
And they who do the Sabbath love,
A happy week will find.

4. P. M.

1 Come, thou Almighty King!
Help us thy name to sing;
Help us to praise!
Father all glorious,
O'er all victorious,
Come, and reign over us,
Ancient of days!

2 Come, thou all-gracious Lord!
By heaven and earth adored,
Our prayer attend!
Come, and thy children bless;
Give thy good word success;
Make thine own holiness
On us descend!

3 Never from us depart!
Rule thou in every heart,
Hence, evermore!
Thy sovereign majesty
May we in glory see,
And to eternity
Love and adore.

5. S. M.

1 Sweet is the task, O Lord,
Thy glorious acts to sing,
To praise thy name, and hear thy word,
And grateful offerings bring.

2 Sweet, at the dawning hour,
Thy boundless love to tell;
And when the night-wind shuts the flower,
Still on the theme to dwell.

3 Sweet, on this day of rest,
To join in heart and voice
With those who love and serve thee best,
And in thy name rejoice.

4 To songs of praise and joy,
Be every Sabbath given,
That such may be our blest employ
Eternally in heaven.

6. S. M.

1 To God the only wise,
Our Saviour and our King,
Let all the saints below the skies
Their humble praises bring.

2 'T is his almighty love,
His counsel and his care,
Preserves us safe from sin and death,
And every hurtful snare.

3 Then all the chosen seed
Shall meet around the throne,
Shall bless the conduct of his grace,
And make his wonders known.

4 To our Redeemer, God,
Wisdom and power belongs,
Immortal crowns of majesty,
And everlasting songs.

7. L. M.

1 WHILE here the throne of grace we seek,
O God, within our spirits speak!
For we will hear thy voice to-day,
Nor turn our hardened hearts away.

2 Speak in thy gentlest tones of love,
Till all our best affections move;
We long to hear no meaner call,
But feel that Thou art all in all.

3 Speak to convince, forgive, console:
Child-like we yield to thy control:
These hearts, too often closed before,
Would grieve thy patient love no more.

8. 7s. M.

1 SUPPLIANT, lo! thy children bend,
Father, for thy blessing now;
Thou canst guard us, guide, defend;
We are weak, almighty thou.

2 With the peace thy word imparts,
Be the taught and teacher blest;
In our lives, and on our hearts,
Father, be thy laws impressed.

3 Shed abroad in every mind,
Light and pardon from above,
Charity for all our kind,
Trusting faith, and holy love.

9. 7s. M.

1 O, GIVE thanks to Him who made
Morning light and evening shade!
Source and Giver of all good, —
Nightly sleep and daily food, —

Quickener of our wearied powers,
Guard of our unconscious hours!

2 O, give thanks for him who came,
In a mortal, suffering frame,
Temple of the Deity; —
Came to bear our souls on high,
In the path himself hath trod,
Leading back his saints to God.

10. L. M.

1 FATHER and Guardian! to thy shrine
The life thou keepest will I bring;
All, great Creator! all is thine;
The heart my noblest offering!

2 The morning light shall see my prayer,
The noonday calm shall know my praise;
And evening's still and fragrant air
My grateful hymn to thee shall raise.

3 So shall sweet thoughts and hopes sublime
My constant inspirations be;
And every shifting scene of time
Reflect, my God, a light from thee!

11. P. M.

1 Father of earth and heaven,
Whose arm upholds creation,
To thee we raise the voice of praise,
And bend in adoration.

2 We praise the power that made us;
We praise the love that blesses;
While every day that rolls away
Thy gracious care confesses.

3 Life is from thee, blest Father;
From thee all breathing spirits;
And thou dost give to all that live
The bliss that each inherits.

4 Day, night, and rolling seasons,
And all that life embraces,
With bliss are crowned, with joy abound,
And claim our thankful praises.

12. 7s. M.

1 Hear ye not a voice from heaven,
To the listening spirit given?
"Children, come!" it seems to say,
"Give your hearts to me to-day."

2 We will give our hearts to thee,
While from pains and sorrows free;
While our day is in its dew,
And the clouds of life are few.

3 Father! now to thee we come,
In our morning's early bloom;
Breathe on us thy grace divine,—
Touch our hearts, and make them thine.

13. 8 & 7s. M.

1 Praise the Lord when blushing morning
Wakes the blossoms wet with dew;
Praise him when revived creation
Beams with beauties fair and new.

2 Praise the Lord, and may his blessing
Guide us in the way of truth;
Keep our feet from paths of error;
Make us holy in our youth.

14. 8 & 7s. M.

1 When the joyous day is dawning,
And the happy light we see,
We who live in life's pure morning,
Father, would remember thee.

2 While in quiet we were sleeping,
Kindly, though we knew it not,
Thou a guardian watch wert keeping:
Never is thy child forgot.

3 Now another day is given,
With thy love may it be blest;
May we learn of thee and heaven,
And prepare for purer rest.

15. C. M.

1 AGAIN, from calm and sweet repose,
I rise to hail the dawn;
Again my waking eyes unclose,
To view the smiling morn.

2 Great God of love! thy praise I'll sing;
For thou hast safely kept
My soul beneath thy guardian wing,
And watched me while I slept.

3 Glory to thee, Eternal Lord!
Oh, teach my heart to pray!
And thy blest Spirit's help afford,
To guide me through the day.

4 Let every thought and word accord
With thy most holy will;
Each deed the precepts of thy word
With pious aim fulfil.

16. 7s. M.

1 Blest Instructor! from thy ways
Who can tell how oft he strays?
Save from error's growth our mind;
Leave not, Lord, one root behind.

2 Purge us from the guilt that lies
Wrapt within our hearts' disguise;
Let us hence, by thee renewed,
Each presumptuous sin exclude.

3 Let our tongues, from error free,
Speak the words approved by thee:
To thine all-observing eyes
Let our thoughts accepted rise.

4 While we thus thy name adore,
And thy healing grace implore,
Blest Instructor! bow thine ear;
God our strength! propitious hear.

17. 8 & 7s. M.

1 Gracious God, our Heavenly Father!
Meet and bless our school, we pray;
As in humble trust we gather,
Teachers, scholars, here to-day.
Every joy, and every blessing,
From thy bounteous hand we own;
May thy love, our souls possessing,
Draw us nearer to thy throne.

2 Weak, imperfect, tempted, erring,
From thy precepts, Lord, we stray;
Let thy spirit, from our wandering,
Bring us back to virtue's way.
Humble, penitent, confiding,
May we rest our hope in thee;
In thy favor, Lord, abiding,
In thy peace and purity.

18. 8 & 7s. M.

1 In the duties now before us
Let us faithfully engage;
Spirit of all truth! be o'er us,
As we search the sacred page:

May the lessons Christ has taught us
All our minds and hearts improve;
And the blessings he has brought us
Wake a strong and holy love.

2 Thankful for the kind protection
Which has blessed us through the week,
Still imploring thy direction,
While we heavenly wisdom seek,
Father! thus, in pure devotion,
Every thought inspired by love,
Gratitude in each emotion,
Would we lift our souls above.

19. C. M.

1 Father! thy children bend the knee;
Give ear unto our prayer!
Let our thanksgiving rise to thee
Upon the morning air.

2 We come, O God, while yet the flower
Of life is but half blown,
To pray thee that its opening hour
May bloom for thee alone!

3 Then, when it fadeth from the earth,
It may in beauty rise,
To bloom where angels have their birth,
In bowers of Paradise.

20. 7 & 6s. M.

1 Go when the morning shineth;
Go when the noon is bright;
Go when the eve declineth;
Go in the hush of night;
Go with pure heart and feeling;
Drive earthly thought away;
And in thy chamber kneeling,
To God in secret pray.

2 Oh! not a joy or blessing
With this can we compare,—
The power that he hath given
To pour our souls in prayer.
Whene'er you meet with sadness,
Before his footstool fall;
Remember, in thy gladness,
His love who gave thee all.

21. 7s. M.

1 Safely through another week
God has brought us on our way;
Let us now a blessing seek,
Waiting in his courts to-day!
Day of all the week the best,
Emblem of eternal rest!

2 Lord, we pray for pardoning grace
In our dear Redeemer's name;
Sin remove, and, in its place,
Give us virtue's purest flame;
Thus from all our sins set free,
May we rest at last with thee.

22. L. M.

1 Great God! and wilt thou condescend
To be my Father and my friend?
I but a child, and thou so high,
The Lord of earth, and air, and sky!

2 Art thou my Father? Let me be
A meek, obedient child to thee;
And try, in every deed and thought,
To serve and please thee as I ought.

3 Art thou my Father? I'll depend
Upon the care of such a friend;
And only wish to do and be
Whatever seemeth good to thee.

4 Art thou my Father? Then, at last,
When all my days on earth are past,
Send down, and take me, in thy love,
To be thy better child above.

23. C. M.

1 It was our Heavenly Father's love
Brought every being forth;
He made the shining worlds above,
And everything on earth.

2 He gives us all our parents dear,
Our teachers kind and true;
And bids us all their precepts hear,
And all they teach us do.

3 God sees and hears us all the day,
And in the darkest night;
He views us when we disobey,
And when we act aright.

4 God hears what we are saying now, —
O, what a wondrous thought!
Our Heavenly Father! teach us how
To love thee as we ought.

24. L. M.

1 He sendeth sun, he sendeth shower;
Alike they 're needful for the flower;
And joys and tears alike are sent,
To give the soul fit nourishment:

As comes to me or cloud or sun,
Father, thy will, not mine, be done!

2 Can loving children e'er reprove
With murmurs whom they trust and love?
Creator! I would ever be
A trusting, loving child to thee:
As comes to me or cloud or sun,
Father, thy will, not mine, be done!

3 O, ne'er will I at life repine!
Enough that thou hast made it mine.
When falls the shadow cold of death,
I yet will sing, with parting breath,
As comes to me or shade or sun,
Father, thy will, not mine, be done!

25. C. M.

1 I THANK the goodness and the grace
Which on my birth have smiled,
And made me, in these Christian days,
A free and happy child.

2 I was not born, as millions are,
Where God was never known,
And taught to pray a useless prayer,
To blocks of wood and stone.

3 My God! I thank thee, who hast planned
  A better lot for me,
And placed me in this Christian land,
  Where I may hear of thee.

4 Help me to serve thee every day,
  Whilst thou shalt give me breath;
And grant that, while on earth I stay,
  I may prepare for death.

26. L. M.

1 O Thou, who hast at thy command
The hearts of all men in thy hand!
Our wayward, erring hearts incline
To have no other will but thine.

2 Our wishes, our desires, control;
Mould every purpose of the soul;
O'er all may we victorious be
That stands between ourselves and thee.

3 Thrice blest will all our blessings be,
When we can look through them to thee;
When each glad heart its tribute pays
Of love, and gratitude, and praise.

27. 11s. M.

1 Our Father in heaven, we hallow thy name,
May thy kingdom holy, on earth be the same;
O, give to us daily our portion of bread;
It is from thy bounty that all must be fed.

2 Forgive our transgressions, and teach us to know
That humble confession that pardons each foe;
Keep us from temptation, from weakness and sin;
And thine be the glory for ever: Amen.

28. L. M.

1 God is so good that he will hear
Whenever children humbly pray;
He always lends a listening year
To what the youngest child may say.

2 His own most holy book declares,
That as a tender father will,
He listens to our lowly prayers,
And what we ask will grant us still.

3 He loves to hear a grateful tongue
Thank him for all his mercies given;
And when on earth his praise is sung,
The cheerful notes are heard in heaven.

29. 9 & 6s. M.

1 Come, rejoice in the Lord;
Come, believe in his word,
And confide in his mercy and grace;
For his throne shall endure,
And his promise be sure,
And in him shall the righteous have peace.

2 O how happy are they,
Who his precepts obey,
And delight in the law of their God;
For their joys shall increase,
And their trials shall cease,
As they enter their holy abode.

30. C. M.

1 None is like God, who reigns above,
So great, so pure, so high;
None is like God, whose name is Love,
And who is always nigh.

2 In all the earth there is no spot
Excluded from his care:
We cannot go where God is not,
For he is everywhere.

3 He is our best and kindest friend,
And guards us night and day:
To all our wants he will attend,
And answer when we pray.

4 O, if we love him as we ought,
And on his grace rely,
We shall be joyful at the thought
That God is always nigh.

31. C. M.

1 THERE 's not a dye that paints the rose,
Or decks the lily fair,
Or tints the humblest flower that blows,
But God has placed it there.

2 There 's not of grass a single blade,
Or leaf of lowliest mien,
Where heavenly skill is not displayed,
And heavenly wisdom seen.

3 There 's not a star whose twinkling light
Illumes the spreading earth;
There 's not a cloud, or dark or bright,
But mercy gave it birth.

4 Then wake, my soul, and sing his name,
And all his praise rehearse,
Who spread abroad earth's glorious frame,
And made the universe.

32. C. M.

1 BEYOND, beyond that boundless sea,
Above that dome of sky,
Farther than thought itself can flee,
Thy dwelling is on high;
Yet dear the awful thought to me,
That thou, my God, art nigh.

2 We hear thy voice when thunders roll
Through the wide fields of air;
The waves obey thy dread control:
Yet still thou art not there.
Where shall I find Him, O my soul,
Who yet is everywhere?

3 O, not in circling depth, or height,
But in the conscious breast,
Present to faith, though veiled from sight,
There does his spirit rest.
O come, thou Presence Infinite,
And make thy creatures blest.

33. L. M.

1 When I look up to yonder sky,
So pure, so bright, so wondrous high,
I think of One I cannot see,
But one who sees and cares for me.

2 'T is he my daily food provides,
And all that I require besides;
And when I close my slumbering eye,
I sleep in peace, for he is nigh.

3 Then surely I should ever love
This gracious God who reigns above;
For very kind indeed is he
To love a little child like me.

34. C. M.

1 There 's not a star whose twinkling light
Illumes the distant earth,
And cheers the solemn gloom of night,
But mercy gave it birth.

2 There 's not a cloud whose dews distil
Upon the parching clod,
And clothe with verdure vale and hill,
That is not sent by God.

3 There 's not a place in earth's vast round,
In ocean deep, or air,
Where skill and wisdom are not found,
For God is everywhere.

4 Around, beneath, below, above,
Wherever space extends,
There Heaven displays its boundless love,
And power with mercy blends.

35. S. M.

1 God, who is just and kind,
Will those who err instruct,
And in the paths of righteousness
Their wandering steps conduct.

2 The humble soul he guides,
Teaches the meek his way,
Kindness and truth he shows to all
Who his just laws obey.

3 Give me the tender heart
That mingles fear with love,
And lead me through whatever path
Thy wisdom shall approve.

4 O, ever keep my soul
From error, shame, and guilt;
Nor suffer the fair hope to fail
Which on thy truth is built.

36. 7s. M.

1 Lo! the lilies of the field!
How their leaves instruction yield!
Hark to Nature's lesson given
By the blessed birds of heaven!
Every bush and tufted tree
Warbles sweet philosophy;
Children, banish care and sorrow,—
God provideth for the morrow.

2 One there lives whose guardian eye
Guides our earthly destiny;
One there lives, who, Lord of All,
Keeps his children when they fall;
Pass we, then, in love and praise,
Trusting him, through all our days,
Free from doubt and faithless sorrow:
God provideth for the morrow.

37. L. M.

1 Among the deepest shades of night,
Can there be one who sees my way?
Yes, God is like the shining light,
That turns the darkness into day.

2 When every eye around me sleeps,
May I not sin without control?
No, for a constant watch he keeps
On every thought of every soul.

3 If I could find some place unknown,
Where human feet have never trod,
Yet there, I could not be alone:
On every side, there would be God.

38. L. M.

1 May I resolve with all my heart,
With all my powers to serve the Lord;
Nor from his precepts e'er depart,
Whose service is a rich reward.

2 O be his service all my joy!
Around let my example shine,
Till others love the blest employ,
And join in labors so divine.

3 Be this the purpose of my soul,
My solemn, my determined choice,
To yield to his supreme control,
And in his kind commands rejoice.

4 O, may I never faint nor tire,
Nor, wandering, leave his sacred ways;
Great God, accept my soul's desire,
And give me strength to live thy praise.

39. C. M.

1 CALM on the listening ear of night
Come heaven's melodious strains,
Where wild Judæa stretches far
Her silver-mantled plains.

2 Celestial choirs from courts above
Shed sacred glories there;
And angels, with their sparkling lyres,
Make music on the air.

3 "Glory to God!" the sounding skies
Loud with their anthems ring;
"Peace to the earth, good-will to men,
From heaven's Eternal King!"

4 Light on thy hills, Jerusalem!
The Saviour now is born!
And bright on Bethlehem's joyous plains
Breaks the first Christmas morn.

40. C. M.

1 In the green fields of Palestine,
And by its winding rills,
Along the Jordan's sacred stream,
And o'er the vine-clad hills, —

2 Once lived and roved the fairest child
That ever blest the earth,
The holiest, the happiest,
And yet of humblest birth.

3 Kindly in all his deeds and words,
And gentle as a dove;
Obedient, affectionate,
His very soul was love.

4 How beautiful his childhood was!
Harmless, and undefiled:
Oh! is it not a blessed thought,
That Christ was once a child!

41. L. M.

1 He lived as none but he has lived,
The wisest Teacher from above;
He died, as none but he has died, —
His every act an act of love.

2 His fervent piety was breathed
To the lone waste, the desert hill,
And in the haunts of men he sought
To do his Heavenly Father's will.

3 He preached the Gospel to the poor;
Beside the couch of anguish stood;
Consoled the sufferer, healed the sick,
And went about still doing good.

42. 7 & 6s. M.

1 Hail to the Lord's anointed!
Great David's greater Son!
Hail in the time appointed,
His reign on earth begun!
He comes to break oppression,
To set the captive free;
To take away transgression,
And rule in equity.

2 He comes with succor speedy
To those who suffer wrong;
To help the poor and needy,
And bid the weak be strong;
To give them songs for sighing;
Their darkness turn to light,
Whose souls, condemned and dying,
Were precious in his sight.

3 He shall come down like showers
Upon the peaceful earth;
And love and joy, like flowers,
Spring in his path to birth;
Before him, on the mountains,
Shall peace, the herald, go;
And righteousness, in fountains,
From hill to valley flow.

43. L. M.

1 How sweetly flowed the Gospel's sound
From lips of gentleness and grace,
When listening thousands gathered round,
And joy and reverence filled the place.

2 From heaven he came; of heaven he spoke;
To heaven he led his followers' way;
Dark clouds of gloomy night he broke,
Unveiling an immortal day.

3 "Come, wanderers, to my Father's home;
Come, all ye weary ones, and rest!"
Yes, sacred Teacher, we will come,
Obey thee, love thee, and be blest.

44. 8, 7, & 4s. M.

1 ONCE was heard the song of children
By the Saviour, while on earth;
Joyful in the sacred temple
Shouts of youthful praise had birth;
And hosannas
Loud to David's Son broke forth.

2 O, though humble is our offering,
Deign accept our grateful lays;
Those from children once proceeding,
Thou didst deem "perfected praise."
Now hosannas,
Saviour, Lord, to thee we raise.

45. 6 & 4s. M.

1 SHEPHERD of tender youth,
Guiding in love and truth
Through devious ways!

Christ our triumphant king!
We come thy name to sing,
And here glad voices bring
To shout thy praise.

2 Thou art our holy Lord!
The all-subduing Word!
Healer of strife!
Thou didst thyself abase,
That from sin's deep disgrace,
Thou mightest save our race,
And give us life.

3 So now, and till we die,
Sound we thy praises high,
And joyful sing;
Infants, and the glad throng
Who to thy Church belong,
Unite and swell the song
To Christ our King.

46. C. M.

1 See Israel's gentle Shepherd stand,
With all-engaging charms;
Hark, how he calls the tender lambs,
And folds them in his arms!

2 Permit them to approach, he cries,
  Nor scorn their humble name;
For 't was to bless such souls as these
  The Lord of angels came;

3 He 'll lead us to the heavenly streams
  Where living waters flow,
And guide us to the fruitful fields
  Where trees of knowledge grow.

4 The feeblest lamb amid the flock
  Shall be its Shepherd's care;
While folded in the Saviour's arms,
  We 're safe from every snare.

47. 7s. M.

1 To thy pastures green and fair,
Saviour, let a child repair;
I will never stray from thee,
But thy fold my home shall be.

2 Like a gentle lamb, I 'll stay
In the meadows fresh and gay;
Peaceful and contented there,
Guarded by my Shepherd's care.

3 By the waters still and clear,
I shall wander without fear;
Happy by my Shepherd's side,
All my wants shall be supplied.

4 Lord, wilt thou my Shepherd be?
Help me, then, to follow thee;
At thy feet myself I cast,
Thee to serve while life shall last.

48. 7s. M.

1 Feeble, helpless, how shall I
Learn to live and learn to die?
Who, O God, my guide shall be?
Who shall lead thy child to thee?

2 Blessed Father, gracious One!
Thou hast sent thy holy Son;
He will give the light I need,
He my trembling steps will lead.

3 Through this world, uncertain, dim,
Let me ever lean on him;
From his precepts wisdom draw,
Make his life my solemn law.

4 Thus in deed, and thought, and word,
Led by Jesus Christ the Lord,
In my weakness, — thus shall I
Learn to live and learn to die.

49. L. M.

1 How many ways the young may find
To be of use, if so inclined!
How many services perform,
If love is earnest, constant, warm!

2 However trifling what we do,
If a good purpose be in view,
Although we should not have success,
Our purpose God will see and bless.

50. L. M.

1 My son, be this thy simple plan:
Serve God, and love thy brother man;
Forget not, in temptation's hour,
That sin lends sorrow double power.

2 Count life a stage upon thy way,
And follow conscience, come what may:
Alike with heaven and earth sincere,
"Fear God, — and know no other fear."

51. C. M.

1 Now that my journey 's just begun,
My road so little trod,
I 'll come before I farther run,
And give myself to God.

2 If all my earthly friends should die,
And leave me mourning here,
Since God can hear the orphan's cry,
O what have I to fear?

3 If I am poor, he can supply
Who has my table spread,
Who feeds the ravens when they cry,
And fills his poor with bread.

4 But, Lord, whatever grief or ill
For me may be in store,
Make me submissive to thy will,
And I would ask no more.

52. 7s. M.

1 Young and happy while thou art,
Not a furrow on thy brow,
Not a sorrow in thy heart,
Seek the Lord, thy Maker, now.

2 In its freshness bring the flower,
While the dew upon it lies,
In the cool and cloudless hour
Of the morning sacrifice.

3 As the first-fruits of the year
Should be offered to the Lord,
So the first-fruits of the heart
On his altar should be poured.

4 Thus the blessing from above
On life's harvest shall be given,
Sown in tears, perhaps, on earth;
Reaped in joyfulness in heaven.

53. S. M.

1 THOU must be born again!
Such was the solemn word
To him who came, not all in vain,
By night to seek the Lord.

2 Thou must be born again!
But not the birth of clay;
The immortal seed must thence obtain
Deliverance unto day.

3 Thou canst not choose but trace
The steps the Master trod,
If once thou feel his truth and grace,
A conscious child of God.

4 The mortal birth is past;
The immortal birth must be;
Seek well, and thou shalt find at last
That blest nativity.

54. C. M.

1 WHAT if the little rain should say,
So small a drop as I
Can ne'er refresh the thirsty fields, —
I'll tarry in the sky?

2 What if a shining beam of noon
Should in its fountain stay,
Because its feeble light alone
Cannot create a day?

3 Doth not each rain-drop help to form
The cool, refreshing shower?
And every ray of light, to warm
And beautify the flower?

4 'T is thus the good each child may do,
When many do their best,
Will help to bring within our view
The glory of the blest.

55. C. M.

1 THINK gently of the erring one!
O, do not thou forget,
However darkly stained by sin,
He is thy brother yet!

2 Speak gently to the erring ones!
Thou yet mayst lead them back,
With holy words, and tones of love,
From misery's thorny track.

3 Forget not thou hast often sinned,
And sinful yet may be;
Deal gently with the erring heart,
As God hath dealt with thee.

56. L. M.

1 FORGIVE thy foes; — nor that alone;
Their evil deeds with good repay;
Fill those with joy who leave thee none,
And kiss the hand upraised to slay.

2 So does the fragrant sandal bow,
In meek forgiveness, to its doom,
And o'er the axe, at every blow,
Sheds in abundance rich perfume.

57. C. M.

1 A LITTLE word in kindness said,
A motion, or a tear,
Has often healed the heart that 's sad,
And made a friend sincere.

2 A word, a look, has crushed to earth
Full many a budding flower,
Which, had a smile but owned its birth,
Would bless life's darkest hour.

3 Then deem it not an idle thing
A pleasant word to speak:
The face you wear, the thoughts you bring
A heart may heal, or break.

58. 7s. M.

1 BLESSED Lord, thy grace impart,
Meek and lowly make my heart;
Poor in spirit may I be,
Clothed with all humility!

2 Simple, teachable, and mild,
As becomes a little child;
Pleased with what my God provides,
Weaned from all the world besides.

3 Father, fix my soul on thee,
Every evil make me flee;
May I seek the things above,
Only happy in thy love!

59. S. M.

1 Blest are the pure in heart,
For they shall see our God;
The secret of the Lord is theirs;
Their soul is his abode.

2 Still to the lowly soul
He doth himself impart,
And for his temple and his throne
Selects the pure in heart.

60. C. P. M.

1 Be it my only wisdom here
To serve the Lord with filial fear,
With loving gratitude.

Superior sense may I display
By shunning every evil way,
  And walking in the good.

2 O may I still from sin depart!
A wise and understanding heart,
  Father, to me be given!
And let me, through thy Spirit, know
To glorify my God below,
  And find my way to heaven.

61. 7s. M.

1 Words are things of little cost,
Quickly spoken, quickly lost;
We forget them, but they stand
Witnesses at God's right hand,
And their testimony bear
For us or against us there.

2 O how often ours have been
Idle words, and words of sin!
Words of anger, scorn, or pride,
Or deceit, our faults to hide,
Envious tales, or strife unkind,
Leaving bitter thoughts behind.

3 Grant us, Lord, from day to day,
Strength to watch, and grace to pray:
May our lips, from sin kept free,
Love to speak and sing of thee;
Till in heaven we learn to raise
Hymns of everlasting praise.

62. 7, 6, & 8s. M.

1 The hours are viewless angels,
That still go gliding by,
And bear each moment's record up
To Him who sits on high.

2 The poison, or the nectar,
Our heart's deep flower-cups yield,
A sample still they gather swift,
And leave us in the field.

3 And as we spend each minute
That God to us has given,
The deeds are known before his throne,
The tale is told in heaven.

4 So teach me, Heavenly Father!
To spend each flying hour,
That, as they go, they may not show
My heart a poison-flower.

63. C. M.

1 Father of mercies! in thy word
What endless glory shines!
For ever be thy name adored
For these celestial lines.

2 Here may the wretched sons of want
Exhaustless riches find;
Riches, above what earth can grant,
And lasting as the mind.

3 O may these heavenly pages be
My ever-dear delight;
And still new beauties may I see,
And still increasing light.

4 Divine Instructor, gracious Lord!
Be thou for ever near;
Teach me to love thy sacred word,
And view my Saviour there.

64. 7s. M.

1 Holy Bible! book divine!
Precious treasure! thou art mine!
Mine to tell me whence I came;
Mine to teach me what I am;

2 Mine to chide me when I rove;
Mine to show a Father's love;
Mine to guide my doubtful feet;
Mine to judge, condemn, acquit;

3 Mine to comfort in distress;
Mine to cheer, sustain, and bless;
Mine to show by living faith
Man can triumph over death;

4 Mine to tell of joys to come;
Mine to lead the spirit home:
O thou precious book divine!
Holy Bible! thou art mine.

65. C. M.

1 UNHEARD the dews around me fall,
And heavenly influence shed;
And silent on this earthly ball
Celestial footsteps tread.

2 Night reigns in silence o'er the pole,
And spreads her gems unheard;
Her lessons penetrate the soul,
Yet borrow not a word.

3 Noiseless the sun emits his fire,
 And pours his golden streams;
And silently the shades retire
 Before his rising beams.

4 O grant my soul an ear to know
 Thy deep and silent voice;
To bend in lowly, filial awe,
 And in thy love rejoice!

66. 7 & 6s. M.

1 In the broad fields of heaven,
 In the immortal bowers,
By life's clear river dwelling,
 Amid undying flowers, —
There hosts of beauteous spirits,
 Fair children of the earth,
Linked in bright bands celestial,
 Sing of their human birth.

2 They sing of earth and heaven;
 Divinest voices rise
To God, their gracious Father,
 Who called them to the skies;
They all are there, — in heaven, —
 Safe, safe, and sweetly blest;
No cloud of sin can shadow
 Their bright and holy rest.

67. C. M.

1 Forth to the land of promise bound,
Our desert path we tread;
God's fiery pillar for our guide,
His Captain at our head.

2 E'en now we faintly see the hills,
And catch their distant blue;
And the bright city's gleaming spires
Rise dimly on our view.

3 There love shall have its perfect work,
And prayer be lost in praise,
And all the servants of our God
Their endless anthems raise.

68. L. M.

1 O, when the hours of life are past,
And death's dark shade arrives at last,
It is not sleep, it is not rest;
'T is glory opening to the blest.

2 Their way to heaven was pure from sin,
And Christ shall there receive them in;
There each shall wear a robe of light,
Like his, divinely fair and bright.

3 There, parted hearts again shall meet,
In union holy, calm, and sweet;
There grief find rest, and never more
Shall sorrow call them to deplore.

4 No storms shall ride the troubled air,
No voice of passion enter there;
But all be peaceful as the sigh
Of evening gales, that breathe and die.

69. C. M.

1 The bird let loose in eastern skies,
When hastening fondly home,
Ne'er stoops to earth her wing, nor flies
Where idle warblers roam;
But high she shoots through air and light,
Above all low delay,
Where nothing earthly bounds her flight
Nor shadows dim her way.

2 So grant me, God, from every care
And stain of passion free,
Aloft, through virtue's purer air
To hold my course to thee;
No sin to cloud, no lure to stay
My soul, as home she springs,
Thy sunshine on her joyful way,
Thy freedom in her wings.

70. C. M.

1 HARK! from that glorious world what songs
Those heavenly voices raise!
Ten thousand thousand infant tongues
Unite in perfect praise.

2 Those are the hymns that we shall know,
If Jesus we obey;
That is the place where we shall go,
If found in wisdom's way.

3 This is the joy we ought to seek,
And make our chief concern;
For this we come, from week to week,
To read, and hear, and learn.

4 Soon will our earthly race be run,
Our mortal frame decay;
Children and teachers, one by one,
Must droop and pass away.

5 Great God, impress the serious thought
This day on every breast,
That both the teachers and the taught
May enter to thy rest.

71. C. M.

1 DEATH rides on every passing breeze,
And lurks in every flower;
Each season has its own disease,
Its peril every hour.

2 Daily we see the rosy light
Of youth's soft cheek decay;
And life depart in sudden night,
Ere scarce has dawned the day.

3 Look downward, then; thy danger know;
Where now thy foot may tread,
List to the warning from below, —
There lie the buried dead.

4 Look upward, too; by faith apply
The truth divinely given;
On Jesus and his word rely,
And fit thy soul for heaven.

72. S. M.

1 O SPIRIT, freed from earth,
Rejoice, thy work is done!
The weary world 's beneath thy feet,
Thou brighter than the sun!

2 Arise, put on the robes
That the redeémèd win;
Now sorrow hath no part in thee,
Thou sanctified within!

3 Awake, and breathe the air
Of the celestial clime!
Awake to love, which knows no change,
Thou who hast done with time!

4 Ascend! thou art not now
With those of mortal birth;
The living God hath touched thy lips,
Thou who hast done with earth!

73. 8 & 7s. M.

1 Peaceful be thy silent slumber,
Peaceful in the grave so low;
Thou no more wilt join our number;
Here no more our songs shalt know.

2 Tears will flow that thou hast left us,
For thy loss we deeply feel;
But 't is God that hath bereft us;
He can all our sorrows heal.

3 Yet again we hope to meet thee,
When the day of life has fled,
Then in heaven with joy to greet thee,
Where no farewell tear is shed.

74. 6 & 5s. M.

1 Saviour, now receive him
To thy bosom mild;
For with thee we leave him,
Blessed, blessed child.

2 Now let thought behold him
In his angel rest,
When those arms enfold him
To a Saviour's breast.

3 We yield but what was given
At thy holy call;
The beautiful to heaven,
Thou who givest all.

75. S. M.

1 Go to thy rest, fair child!
Go to thy dreamless bed,
While yet so gentle, undefiled,
With blessings on thy head.

2 Because thy smile was fair,
Thy lip and eye so bright,
Because thy loving cradle-care
Was such a fond delight,—

3 Shall love, with weak embrace,
Thy upward wing detain?
No! gentle angel, seek thy place
Amid the cherub train.

76. C. M.

1 WHY do we mourn departing friends,
Or shake at death's alarms?
'T is but the voice that Jesus sends,
To call them to his arms.

2 Why should we tremble to convey
Their bodies to the tomb?
'T is but the consecrated way
To their eternal home.

77. 8 & 7s. M.

1 CEASE, ye mourners, cease to languish
O'er the grave of those you love;
Pain and death and night and anguish
Enter not the world above.

2 While our silent steps are straying,
Lonely, through night's deepening shade,
Glory's brightest beams are playing
Round the happy Christian's head.

78. L. M.

1 Great God, we own that mighty hand
By which, supported, still we stand;
The opening year thy mercy shows;
That mercy crowns it till it close.

2 With grateful hearts the past we own;
The future, all to us unknown,
We to thy guardian care commit,
And peaceful leave before thy feet.

3 In scenes exalted or depressed,
Thou art our joy and thou our rest;
Thy goodness all our hopes shall raise,
Adored through all our changing days.

79. C. M.

1 Awake, O God, my careless heart
Its great concerns to see,
That I may act the Christian part,
And give the year to thee.

2 So shall their course more grateful roll,
If future years arise,
Or this shall bear my waiting soul
To joy beyond the skies.

80. S. M.

1 God of our fathers, hear,
Thou everlasting friend!
While we, as on life's utmost verge,
Our souls to thee commend.

2 Of all the pious dead
May we the footsteps trace,
Till with them, in the land of light,
We dwell before thy face.

81. 6 & 5s. M.

1 Summer days are coming,
Winter days are gone;
Merry birds are singing
In the flowery lawn.

2 Now the sun is shining,
With his cheerful rays;

O, how very pleasant
Are these summer days!

3 Honey-bees are gathering
Sweets from all the flowers;
Ever, ever busy
All the sunny hours.

4 May we learn the lesson
To be busy too;
Ever, ever seeking
Useful work to do.

5 God, our great Creator,
Gave these summer days;
May our hearts and voices
Join to give him praise.

82. S. M.

1 THE freshly blooming flowers
To thee sweet offerings bear;
And cheerful birds in shady bowers
Sing forth thy tender care.

2 The fields on every side,
The trees on every hill,
The glorious sun, the rolling tide,
Proclaim thy wonders still.

3 But trees and fields and skies
Still praise a God unknown;
For gratitude and love can rise
From living hearts alone.

4 These living hearts of ours
Thy holy name would bless;
The blossoms of all nature's flowers
Would please our Father less.

83. 7 & 6s. M.

1 THERE cometh o'er the spirit,
With each returning year,
The thought that thou, the Father,
Art ever to us near;
With hope of life dispelling
The death that winter brought,
And flowers and fruits foretelling,
With fragrant beauty fraught.

2 'T is this which calls thy children
In sweet accord to raise,
Beneath thy blue-domed temple,
One general hymn of praise
To thee, the ever living,
The universal King,

Who never ceasest giving
  Each good and perfect thing.

3 The streamlet from the mountain,
  It speaketh, Lord, of thee,
As from its snow-capped fountain
  It rushes to the sea;
The gentle dew descending,
  And cloud's refreshing shower, —
O God, our Heavenly Father,
  All, all proclaim thy power.

84. C. M.

1 HERE like the birds, that wander free,
  Warbling their woodland lays,
We, Heavenly Father, sing to thee
  Our grateful song of praise.

2 The happy minstrels of the air,
  That on thy bounty live,
With songs repay thy constant care, —
  'T is all that they can give.

3 But we can give the loving heart,
  And lift our thoughts above,
Can learn that thou our Father art,
  And feel that thou art love.

4 A table in the wilderness
Of old thy bounty spread,
When manna dropped, the tribes to bless
That cried to thee for bread.

5 For us kind friends a feast prepare
Beneath this woodland shade;
Scarce better could thy children fare
Whose food the manna made.

6 Never, like them, may we be heard
To murmur or repine;
Still may we heed thy holy word,
And form our wills to thine.

85. 7 & 6s. M.

1 We meet again in gladness,
And thankful voices raise;
To God, our Heavenly Father,
We tune our grateful praise:
His own kind hand hath kept us
Through all the changing year;
His love it is that brings us
Again to worship here.

2 We thank him for the Sabbath,
This day of holy rest;
And for the blessed Bible,
The book the good love best;
For Sabbath schools and teachers,
To us in kindness given,
To guide us in the pathway
That leads to joys in heaven.

3 We thank him for our country,
The land our fathers trod;
For liberty of conscience,
And right to worship God.
O Lord, our Heavenly Father,
Accept the praise we bring,
And tune our hearts and voices
Thy glorious name to sing.

4 Soon may thy gracious sceptre
Extend to every land,
And all as willing subjects
Submit to thy command.
Send forth the gospel tidings,
And hasten on the day
When every isle and nation
Shall own the Saviour's sway.

86. L. M.

1 WHAT thanks, O God, to thee are due,
That thou didst plant our fathers here,
And watch and guard them as they grew,
A vineyard to the planter dear!

2 Thy kindness to our fathers shown,
In weal or woe, through all the past,
Their grateful sons, O God, shall own
While here their name and race shall last.

87. 6 & 4s. M.

1 GOD bless our native land!
Firm may she ever stand
Through storm and night!
When the wild tempests rave,
Ruler of wind and wave!
Do thou our country save,
By thy great might.

2 For her our prayer shall rise
To God above the skies;
On him we wait;
Thou who hast heard each sigh,
Watching each weeping eye,
Be thou for ever nigh;—
God save the State!

88. 6 & 4s. M.

1 My country, 't is of thee,
Sweet land of liberty,
Of thee I sing.
Land where my fathers died,
Land of the pilgrims' pride,
From every mountain side
Let freedom ring.

2 My native country, thee, —
Land of the noble, free, —
Thy name, — I love;
I love thy rocks and rills,
Thy woods and templed hills;
My heart with rapture thrills
Like that above.

3 Let music swell the breeze,
And ring from all the trees
Sweet freedom's song:
Let mortal tongues awake;
Let all that breathe partake;
Let rocks their silence break, —
The sound prolong.

4 Our fathers' God, to thee,
Author of liberty,
To thee we sing:

Long may our land be bright
With freedom's holy light;
Protect us by thy might,
Great God, our King.

89. 8 & 7s. M.

1 FATHER! grant us now thy blessing;
Smile upon us from above;
Let us all, pure hearts possessing,
Fill our lives with deeds of love.

2 Make us gentle, kind, and lowly;
Teach us, Father, by thy word,
How we may be good and holy,
Like to Jesus Christ our Lord.

90. C. M.

1 How pleasant thus, to dwell below
In fellowship of love;
And though we part, 't is bliss to know
The good shall meet above.

2 The children who have loved the Lord,
Shall hail their parents there;
And teachers gain the rich reward
Of all their toil and care.

3 Then let us each, in strength divine,
Still walk in wisdom's ways;
That we, with those we love, may join
In never-ending praise.

91. 7s. M.

1 THANKS to thee, before we part,
Father, rise from every heart,
For the blessed Sabbath, given
To prepare our souls for heaven.

2 Give the teaching of this hour
O'er our lives a guiding power;
Deep impress thy saving truth
On the wavering heart of youth.

3 Guide and Guardian be to each,
Till that safer home we reach
Where — sweet Sabbaths never o'er —
We shall meet and part no more.

92. C. M.

1 THY gracious aid, great God, impart,
To give thy word success;
Write all its precepts on the heart,
And deep its truths impress.

2 O speed our progress in the way
That leads to joy on high,
Where knowledge grows without decay,
And love shall never die.

93. 7s. M.

1 As the sun's enlivening eye
Shines on every place the same,
So the Lord is always nigh
To the souls that love his name.

2 When they move at duty's call,
He is with them by the way;
He is ever with them all, —
Those who go, and those who stay.

3 For a season called to part,
Let us, then, ourselves commend
To the gracious eye and heart
Of our ever-present Friend.

4 Father, hear our humble prayer!
Tender Shepherd of thy sheep,
Let thy mercy and thy care
All our souls in safety keep.

94. 8s. & 7s. M.

1 Lo! the day of rest declineth;
Gather fast the shades of night;
May the sun that ever shineth
Fill our souls with heavenly light.

2 Softly now the dew is falling;
Peace o'er all the scene is spread;
On his children, meekly calling,
Purer influence God will shed.

3 While thine ear of love addressing,
Thus our parting hymn we sing,
Father, give thine evening blessing;
Fold us safe beneath thy wing.

95. 7s. M.

1 Softly fades the twilight ray
Of the holy Sabbath day;
Gently as life's setting sun,
When the Christian's course is run.

2 Night her solemn mantle spreads
O'er the earth, as daylight fades;
All things tell of calm repose
At the holy Sabbath's close.

3 Father, may our Sabbaths be
Days of peace and joy in thee;
Till in heaven our souls repose,
Where the Sabbaths ne'er shall close.

96. 8 & 7s. M.

1 On the dewy breath of even
Thousand odors mingling rise,
Borne like incense up to heaven,—
Nature's evening sacrifice.

2 With her balmy offerings blending,
Let our glad thanksgivings be—
To thy throne, O Lord, ascending—
Incense of our hearts to thee.

3 Thou, whose favors without number
All our days with gladness bless!
Let thine eye, that knows not slumber,
Guard our hours of helplessness.

4 Then, though conscious we are sleeping
In the outer courts of death,
Safe beneath a Father's keeping,
Calm we rest in placid faith.

97. 7s. M.

1 Slowly, by God's hand unfurled,
Down around the weary world
Falls the darkness; O how still
Is the working of his will!

2 Mighty Spirit, ever nigh!
Work in me as silently;
Veil the day's distracting sights;
Show me heaven's eternal lights.

98. C. M.

1 Before I close my eyes in sleep,
Lord, hear my evening prayer;
And deign a helpless child to keep
By thy protecting care.

2 The little birds, that sing all day,
In many a leafy wood,
By thee are clothed in plumage gay,—
By thee supplied with food.

3 And when at night they cease to sing,
By thee protected still,
Their young ones sleep beneath their w
Secure from every ill.

4 Thus wilt thou guard, with gracious arm,
The couch whereon I lie,
And keep thy child from every harm
Beneath thy watchful eye.

99. C. M.

1 How beautiful the setting sun!
The clouds, how bright and gay!
The stars, appearing one by one,
How beautiful are they!

2 And when the moon climbs up the sky,
And sheds her gentle light,
And hangs her crystal lamp on high,
How beautiful is night!

3 And can it be, that I 'm possessed
Of something brighter far?
Glows there a light within this breast
Outshining every star?

4 Yes! 'T is the soul that God has given:
Sin may its lustre dim,
While goodness bears it up to heaven,
And leads it back to him.

100. L. M.

1 From all that dwell below the skies,
Let the Creator's praise arise;
Let the Redeemer's name be sung,
Through every land, by every tongue.

2 Eternal are thy mercies, Lord!
Eternal truth attends thy word!
Thy praise shall sound from shore to shore,
Till suns shall rise and set no more.

INDEX OF FIRST LINES.

THE END.

www.ingramcontent.com/pod-product-compliance
Lightning Source LLC
LaVergne TN
LVHW010239110826
845151LV00004B/1339

9781425525040